Growing Old in America: Notes from a Codger

Some thoughts on what it means to be aging in this time and place

By John Bolinger

Preface

There are so many ways to look at aging. America happens to be one of the most difficult places to grow old, despite the nation's relative affluence in the world. Other cultures honor and even revere their elderly as our American Indians did. Though Eskimos used to place their elderly upon ice floes and send them out to sea, our way of dealing with the elderly seems to be rendering them invisible, which may actually be worse than putting them on traveling ice floes. American deification of youth, an attitude going back to the 1920's, has created false assumptions about what it means to grow older, and as time passes, those assumptions become less and less accurate. The old stereotypes of rocking chairs, playing checkers, wearing dentures that don't fit, and being generally unaware of modernity on any level are still common misconceptions, which are outdated at best. Television messages about people who fall down and can't get up serve only to fuel this attitude that "old people" are useless burdens. In a world where wisdom and experience are less valued than fast cars, fashionable clothes, and looking sexy, the elderly suffer from widely accepted prejudice about not being able to live up to society's standards of worth. It's really a story not unlike that of women and Blacks fighting for the respect and even admiration that they have always deserved. Finally it may be that the stiff, outmoded and artificial standards themselves are the problem.

Maybe we need to redefine even what we mean by "elderly." The definition continues to change over time and to be different for each individual. Lifespans continue to increase. I turned sixty-eight this year, which entitles me to call myself a "codger," which the American Heritage Dictionary defines as "an old or somewhat eccentric man." The number sixty-eight qualifies me to be called "old" by most of society, and my writing books certainly renders me eccentric, so I'm covered by both issues in the definition. I'm willing to wear the label of "codger" proudly, as long as it is understood that age alone doesn't merit judgment, and that I reserve the right to show who I am based upon what I might be about beyond the usual criteria of speed and profit.

James, one of my friends, will turn ninety-five next January. His piano playing can still leave a keyboard in flames, and he's a better bowler than I. His wit, memory, kindness, and general knowledge of the world I would match against most people forty or fifty years his junior. He remains an inspiration to me and to so many others, especially those over the age of sixty, because we see in him what we would like to be as we grow older. His keen interest in and knowledge of current events could put most other people far younger to shame. He is, for example, an avid reader of and subscriber to The New Yorker magazine (and gives me the issues as he finishes them). Of course, when you're ninety-four, almost everyone else is "young" or at least "younger." James has lived through the Jazz Age, The Great Depression, World War II, the Korean War, the terrifying years of the McCarthy era during the 1950's, Vietnam, the social upheavals of the 1960's and 1970's, and seventeen presidents of the United States, not to mention the extraordinary developments in technology since he was born in 1920.

James has seen so many cultural fads come and go over the past ninety-four years that he seems amusingly tolerant of everything from Hip Hop to rap and tattoos. He knows that taste continues to evolve and sometimes repeat itself. He smiles at most of it. The reader will find that I am less accepting of modernity than James is and that my suspicions about the prevalence of technology in our time are far more filled with criticism than those of James, who often laughs when I complain that the world is moving too fast.

At last I want to express some views on aging from those of us who can no longer be classified as young or even middle-aged (at least by society's definitions). We still serve a purpose, are not invisible, and we are growing in numbers as never before in history. Growing old is something most of us must face sooner or later, but it need not be the curse that our youth-centered culture would have us believe.   John Bolinger

Chapter 1: Shared Stories

The British, Victorian prime minister, Benjamin Disraeli, considered himself to be a serious traveler. He said, "I have seen more than I remember and remember more than I have seen." That statement is a most cogent one in terms of life itself being a kind of journey, and I think it applies very well to how writers see the world, the one in which they travel physically, and the ones which they create through their authorship of stories, essays, poems, and books.

Life is a kind of time machine, but which travels in only one direction, at its own pace from birth to the grave, taking most of us through a series of visits to childhood, phases of other periods, like adolescence, marriage, careers, raising children, retirement, old age, and death. Along the way, we make mental notes of people, places, sounds, smells, tastes, and other sensations, happy and sad, that we store away in those caverns of memory that become not only the sources of what we think, feel, and write, but of who we are.

The writer perhaps remembers (at least subconsciously) more detail from his experiences, but beyond that, he arranges them in patterns that express genuine human emotions through fears, hopes, and dreams that we all somehow share as a species. Also, the details in the writer's mind may be rearranged, accommodating needs of plot, emotional catharsis, and general design of the composition. Such recollection of detail comes from real life, but it is often put into new combinations and different orders, as in dreams. Writers also tend to create details, though they are not the only people to do this. Children are quite good at it too.

Everyone has a story to tell, and if we all had the chance to tell our stories (from the highest Nobel laureate to the vilest criminal), the world would probably be a much more peaceful place, because it would be based upon mutual understanding. In that sense, we are all writers, each with a tome of experience internalized over however many years he or she has lived, even though that tome may never become an actual printed book. Sometimes, walking down a street, riding in a plane, train, or buying groceries, I will look at another person briefly, wondering what his or her story might be, and I have the deep feeling that there would be no story that could be uninteresting if I could know all its connections and details. Each of us is a combination of all the experiences he has ever had, every sensation, every encounter, every recollection, every heartache, and every joy. Imagine how different the world would be if everyone could share his complete story with everyone else. Perhaps that may be at least a part of what heaven is.

Chapter 2: Cusp of the Old Year…2010

Today is Christmas Eve. In some ways, I still feel the way I did as a child in the 1950's, in awe of this season of transformation, and in other ways I have learned to savor this time in terms of looking at the past, enjoying its recollections, and then letting go too.   It is certainly a time for personal and family traditions that help to anchor us in an ever-changing, increasingly impersonal world of electronics that promises us speed and human connection but which at last gives us still more distance between us and others, and a shallow, abbreviated text message of what we once loved, like a sumptuous meal condensed into some flavorless capsule. All the more reason to cherish a time of year when, for reasons that transcend both religion and commercialism, we confront an emotionalreality based upon everything we have been and everything we would like to become.

Think of that holiday card you have received from an old friend from whom you haven't heard in a long time, the signature alone summoning happy memories of times gone by. That occurrence is most common at this time of year, because we have almost a collective acceptance of genuine sentiment, which many are too embarrassed to allow during any other season. There is still something childlike and innocent about this time of year that takes us back to a naive but heartfelt joy in being with those we love and remembering those who are gone. Zuzu's petals (IT'S A WONDERFUL LIFE), and Rosebud (Citizen Kane) are such powerful symbols of what we once saw and valued so clearly as children. Maybe that's why children are still at the hub of all that is Christmas, from the Christ child in his manger crib, to the face of a child on Christmas morning opening his first gift. Everything about this season says, "Hey! It's OK. Go ahead and feel deeply. Forgive those who have treated you badly and don't be afraid to show unbridled kindness and generosity to those you love." We, like Ebenezer Scrooge, can be transformed as at no other time of the year. We can become more appreciative of what we have and of what we can give. It's a miraculous time.

For us adults at this time of year there is a

strong feeling of time passing, as the clock ticks toward January first, when we let go of our sentimental views of past days (at least for a while) and replace our memories with hopes of better and more productive days that lie ahead, doing better at work, losing a few pounds through sheer will power, cleaning that hall closet, writing to those old friends we haven't heard from for a long time. We find a new chance to do well and to accomplish goals, however small.

Don't be afraid or embarrassed to let the season enfold you or to allow yourself to enfold it. The rewards are incalculable.

Chapter 3: Dear Everybody: Thoughts on E-Mail versus Traditional Letters

Every once in a while I can feel myself aging, not just by looking in the mirror to see more silver hair, but also because I feel a lag in my attempts to keep up, even remotely, with technology and what the rest of the world delights in calling "progress."

We live in a time that increasingly stresses speed and instant gratification. Though I'm for whatever makes life easier, I know that such strides inevitably encourage us to become lazier and to leave behind certain intangibles, like thoughtfulness, patience, and graciousness. I still have letters written to me by my maternal grandmother in her own

15

hand. The first of these was sent to me on my ninth birthday, but all her letters, right through my years at college were written with a pen and bottled ink upon stationery, a gold border around each page. Reading them again is like delving into history, or like seeing light that left stars eons ago and is just now arriving to illuminate the night sky. I can count on one hand the people I know personally, who still mail hand-written letters, which for me have become something of an archaic luxury in a world where technology seems to be reducing language to an efficient but artificial Esperanto of what it once was. It saddens me at times to remember the books on language usage, grammar, and composition I used as a student and then as a teacher and to see so much eloquence and grace of the mother tongue often funneled down to the polyester communication of a text message.

I can't remember any e-mails or text messages that would stay in my head for more than an hour. They can be lauded for their spontaneity and the fact that postage stamps are not required (though such communication is certainly not free of charge). The internet seems at times to be a huge conveyor belt of gang mail sent indiscriminately by some people, piles of it forwarded, faceless, impersonal messages that senders believe somehow will inspire or entertain the recipients. The sheer volume of these e-mails reduces their value, as they all melt together at last into a mind-numbing flow of messages that begin to resemble TV commercials.

Letters used to be mailed on folded sheets of paper, sealed with hot wax until around 1840 in England, when envelopes came into vogue. Time was taken to compose messages that cost money and that would take days or even weeks to arrive at their destinations. Contemplation was more evident in communications that could not be shot back and forth with great speed, as in conversation. I remember in the 1950's through the 1970's the anticipation of waiting for the postman to deliver responses to letters I'd written and mailed. There was a sense of waiting and reward in writing that was not quite as casual as it is in e-mails today. I must add, however, that computers and e-mail are not responsible for the "death" of letter writing. It was, I believe, the telephone that was responsible for that if, indeed, letter writing is dead.

So much of what is forwarded in e-mails is undocumented drivel or just plain propaganda for one political cause or another, with absolutely shameless disregard for facts or any sort of certification. Of course, this was undoubtedly part of handwritten communication too, but it's so easy now to send libelous or fact-free messages fluttering by the hundreds or thousands into cyberspace, that one wonders what is true and what has been twisted to fit whatever ideology the sender has embraced. I see this sort of thing daily on FaceBook, when people grandstand for their political views on the extreme left or right. Just because it's on the internet, doesn't mean it's true or hasn't been modified to fit a sender's personal agenda, no matter how outrageous.

As anachronistic as they seem, I still miss personal, handwritten thank-you notes and carefully crafted letters. That nostalgia is just one of the things that may render me a fuddy-duddy, who still uses a fountain pen and stationery which for many will seem as outmoded as horse-drawn carriages, outhouses, and library paste.

When President Ronald Reagan announced that he had Alzheimer's, he did it with ink on paper himself. I doubt that the impact of that note in its quivering script would have had the same power as a fax or a letter typed on White

House stationery by an aide. I think too about heartbreaking, handwritten notes by dying soldiers during the American Civil War, final letters, stained with blood of the writers, letters held dear for generations by families of those courageous young men. There is something about holding a letter that was physically touched by the writer and written with some care by hand. I have an old hat box of over a hundred letters written by my father between 1941 and 1945 to my mother while he was stationed in London and then in the South Pacific during World War II. Holding those letters in my hand more than seventy years after their composition is indescribable. My mother, when she was dating my father in the late 1930's and early 1940's, would mail him letters scented with lilac or lavender.

Such letters, even unscented ones, are sensory experiences. E-mails are not. Such an argument is used also by people, who prefer reading traditional leather-bound or paperback books over eBooks. As a true techno-civilization, we haven't yet gone over completely to "the dark side." There are still ink pens, pencils, and stationery in most stores, obviously because there are still enough people using them to make sales lucrative enough to continue. In that case, maybe I need not panic until I'm a

centenarian, who might appear on the evening news as an ancient reminder of a time when people actually wrote letters by hand, even saving in hat boxes and desk drawers the ones that were important or dear enough not to be deleted.

Finally, it may be that I long for the polite salutations and closings of letters we used to write by hand. Maybe my ego simply enjoyed seeing my name as the principal recipient of communication, not just one of fifty other names in or out of blind copy. The next generation will be different at least in the sense that they will be the first in many centuries not even to need cursive writing, which is now being eliminated in many American schools. Future power outages and dead batteries may mean at least temporary cancelations of even printed communication.

Chapter 4: Aging Cycles

My Partner just endured a back surgery last week that involved vertebrae fusions and Stenosis treatment. The aftermath of pain from this is probably unimaginable to most of us, who have been fortunate not to have suffered back issues. There is now enough titanium inside Jim to render him practically bionic. Any other metal would pick up FM radio stations. Having seen his previous X-rays, I would have given the diagnosis that Jim had swallowed an entire Erector Set, based upon the hardware that was placed there before. His subsequent surgery was apparently part medical and part architectural.

I had to fill several prescriptions at Walgreens

for medications, and as I sat in the pleasant little waiting area, my anxieties over what Jim was undergoing gradually but temporarily subsided, as the only sound in the place was a recording of Mary Travers of "Peter, Paul, and Mary," singing "Leavin' on a Jet Plane." There were others in chairs waiting for their prescriptions to be filled, people with gray hair. I smiled as I thought of our all being from the same generation, and I was able to read on their faces a kind of nostalgia as we all listened to that music from almost fifty years before, music that was perhaps taking us all back for a few moments to the days of our youth, when we were in high school or college. Without having to speak, we were sharing a collective history together.

"I'm leavin' on a jet plane.

I don't know when I'll be back again..."

As my name was called to pick up the prescriptions, a recording of The Mamas and the Papas played, "California Dreamer." It was almost as though Walgreens knew that their clientele at the prescription counter would be people our age, those who need a little extra help in coping with the painful reality of aging. Then I made my way out the automatic doors into the parking lot and back into the present world, the" real" world, that eventually the young of today will remember nostalgically too, perhaps while sitting in a room in some future Walgreens, waiting for their own prescriptions to be filled, looking back at what it was like to be young, and sharing that bliss silently with others from their own time. The winter of one's life isn't so bad if only he can recall sometimes those warm, sunny days of being young.

"All the leaves are brown and the sky is grey.

I've been for a walk on a winter's day.

I'd be safe and warm if I was in L.A.

California dreaming on such a winter's day."

Chapter 5: A Few Words on Popular Music

My thoughts today on current pop music would probably insult the teenagers whose tastes lean heavily in the direction of songs that are now heard almost everywhere we go. My concern, however, over offending the young is minimized by the fact that it will be highly unlikely that any teens would be reading this book. Also, I believe strongly that anyone who listens regularly to such music is probably devoid of the tenderness of spirit to feel or even recognize an insult when it's hurled at him. Yes, I'm horribly intolerant in this matter, especially when I'm forced to listen to rubbish that so many call "music" in our public places.

Last Wednesday while bowling at a local place for two hours, I listened, however unwillingly, to song after song at volumes strong enough to shatter steel beams, every one of the songs in common time with the same mind-numbing tempo and repetitively mindless lyrics, to the point that my brain began to feel immobilized by the utter dullness of the listening experience. I'd like to blame my bad bowling scores on the music, but that would be going too far, I suppose. Without earplugs I felt at the mercy of the dreadful music and being forced to hear what was surely more a phenomenon of electronic sound enhancement and technology than of actual musical talent or originality of performance. The term "performing artist" is way overused nowadays.

Maybe we've reached the point where we really don't want to be stimulated mentally by background music but rather deadened by it as robotic accompaniment to whatever else we're doing. I guess we've all become multi-taskers anyway. That kind of pop music seems paralyzed by a sameness that desensitizes life in a way that texting and cellphones do. Primitively inarticulate, the music becomes as pervasive as a stupefying companion uttering the same word over and over again until it loses all meaning.

I'm old enough to remember that our pop music of the 1950's through the 1980's could certainly be dumb too, but at least it didn't all sound exactly the same. I've come to that juncture in life, where I can hear several pop songs in a row and not be able to tell they weren't all done by the same performer. Part of that is due to the aging process and my remembering fondly the music and lyrics by people like the Gershwins, Jerome Kern, Harold Arlen, Cole Porter, Oscar Hammerstein, Jules Stein, Stephen Sondheim, and Irving Berlin, but a big part of it too is that much of the pop music of today is just inane. From a sense, however, of compassion, pity, or condolence, I won't mention any of its specific names.

Chapter 6: Gray Hair and Aging

We live in a nation that has a terrible phobia of aging. Our youth-centered values saturate the media on everything from cars to clothing and entertainment. Since the 1920's, "the age of gin and flappers," we have increasingly shunned the idea of growing old, even if gracefully, and the result is that youth and their aged counterparts have become more separated than ever before.

In centuries before the 20th, young people mingled more with their elders, because often grandparents ended up living with their children, so that the household was a blend of generations. Also, travel was quite a different challenge in that riding a horse or taking a carriage was not usually a spur of the moment decision. Entertainment was at home, whenever there was leisure time. Music, games, and conversation were much more multi-generational, out of necessity. Nowadays, teenagers seem desperate to escape their homes to be anywhere but with their older family members. Though there has always been the phenomenon of youth seeking its own identity through distancing itself from elders during teen years, that separation was not as pronounced until the 20th Century. It has now become almost a chasm.

Perhaps behind our terror of growing "old" is a fear of death itself, which in our time seems, to many, more of a finality than in previous centuries, when an afterlife was more of a reality in general belief than in modern times. Today our association with all things "chic" are connected in some way with the beauty, energy, and health of being young. Too few images of contented elders are shown in the media. We tend to see being aged as the end of a journey instead of a journey in itself, one that can provide time, not just for rest, but for further exploration on one's own terms and at one's own pace.

I resent ads that speak of getting rid of gray hair as though it's some kind of cancer that will prevent participation in the modern world and any kind of happiness or respect by others. People with gray hair are not lepers. This morning I read about studies being done in England and Germany toward a "cure" for gray hair. Cure? Growing old is not a disease, but the article suggested that it was, and that not having gray hair would bring back a flaming youth and happiness that would otherwise not be possible. What rubbish! Sexiness is wonderful in its place, but so are things like experience, character, and wisdom, all of which gray hair can represent. And who says that someone with silver hair can't be sexy anyway?

Almost all the people I know personally, who have gray or white hair are comfortable, stable friends, who have taken care of themselves and are enjoying their golden years. I include myself among those who are enjoying their "declining" years, still in excellent health, and with goals and projects that keep their creativity and joy of being alive realities. My hair is silver and on its way to being snow white eventually. That fact will never keep me up nights worrying that something has been

lost. In fact, I know that much has been

gained.

Chapter 7: Growing Old in America

Growing old isn't something that happens overnight any more than an eight-hundred-pound man looking in the mirror one morning while shaving and saying to himself, "Gee, I've really let myself go!" Aging is so gradual that we are aware of it only at intervals when we notice more silver in our hair, more joint pain, unsightly shifts in weight, like sand slowly filling the bottom half of an hourglass, or the increasing phenomenon of forgetting simple but important things more frequently, like where the car keys are, or one of the hundred passwords we need to survive the internet. Most of these changes are minor annoyances that come and go, but they accumulate over time until one morning in just the right light, the mirror throws back an image of someone we hardly recognize in terms of who we remember having been.

Romanticizing the present becomes more difficult, so we begin to embellish the past, or at least to think of it as superior to the "now." This common practice of honoring "the good old days" may be a human trait all over the world, but in America, it is something that stems from our often irrational worship of youth itself. Our obsession with being and staying young is where so much of our energy and money go in this country. I'm not sure if this comes from our terror of losing our independence, our looks, or our health, but it is perhaps from what may be our greatest but mostly unspoken fear, that of death itself, which Jeffrey Schrank, in the early 1970's,

said would become our next taboo, the one
taking precedence over all other taboos, one
so horrible that it remains unspoken until the
last moments of having to deal with it.
Elizabeth Kubler-Ross understood the
necessity of seeing death as something natural
and inevitable, but it is something we shun
perhaps because there is something so
apparently final about the idea of "shuffling
off this mortal coil." Maybe the principal
reason we have religion is that it helps to
cushion the reality of death's inevitability by
providing hope for defeating the final source
of individual and group extinction.

The fear we have of death may help to explain
why models in fashion ads are becoming more
and more adolescent so that occasionally
those ads display evening gowns worn by what

appear to be twelve-year-olds. Though they usually don't even look that healthy, these symbolic youths give us what may be the illusion of greater distance from death. They give us time to spare.

The youth cult in our country began probably in the 1920's after the Great War, which decimated the youth of Europe and to some extent, that of our own country. Our preoccupation with being "young" survives unabated, even as the Baby Boomers from World War II continue to age, and advertising in all its forms perpetuates the image of aging as some sort of disease for which the only cures are exercise, cosmetics, and Botox. We're a nation of happy illusions when it comes to aging. Eventually, however, geriatrics will become perhaps the most important field of endeavor we have in our struggle to find that life can be rich and rewarding without shame or stigma in all its phases, even the final one.

There is a comment I read recently by the TV writer and actress, Roseanne Barr. It is certainly a feminist viewpoint, but I like the energy and determination of what she said. There is a fighting spirit in her words that all of us as older people need to feel from time to time.

"I am old now: gray, wrinkled, tired, and bloated, and my joints ache too. But, I am ready to come into my full destiny, as my childhood dreams predicted, as a Neo-Amazonian Pirate Queen of my own vessel, firing cannonballs at the worldwide culture of patriarchy in the name of all that does not suck."

Chapter 8: Notes from a Codger about Electronics...

One day during the 1980's I was in my dad's study, and he was showing me his new Commodore computer. He said to me then that the wave of the future was going to be electronic devices for communication that in twenty years would make the world as we knew it unrecognizable. Little did I know at that time how accurate Dad's prediction was.

I seem to live in a perpetual struggle between my appreciation of and my aversion to technology. Electronic strides in computers and cellphones are being made so fast that I have hardly enough time to turn around before the next upgrade, update, or replacement is required. I use the word "required" in this instance only in the sense that we are all made to feel out of date if something is not brand new. For example, my cellphone is an old flip phone, small, uncomplicated, and unencumbered by a catalog of "apps" I would never use anyway. It doesn't play music, show movies, make coffee, or toast muffins. It sends and receives calls efficiently with a long battery life. That's all. Other features for the newest phones seem as silly as those on a future electric razor that might include apps for doing yard work too. There's a limit to my sense of humor about these things.

There have been times recently when while I was using my cellphone in public, that people stared at me as though I were wearing a powdered wig and buckled shoes. I like my

44

1997 car, my 1968 electric coffee pot, and my 1965 toaster, all in perfect condition, and the money I might otherwise have spent on newer versions (to impress the world around me?) is in my bank account instead. Almost any replacements would probably have been made in China, so it's not as though I'm personally stifling the American economy by not feeling obligated to "keep up."

The phenomenon that continues to fascinate and repulse me at once is our national obsession with texting, that abbreviation of what we used to call communication and even conversation. What is there about this technical sensation that can turn people into robots, keeping them chained to the beep or other signal that the next message has arrived? Egotism? Texting has fostered a kind of modern rudeness that Robert Heinlein and Isaac Asimov would have loved to satirize. I've been in homes where family members in the same room were texting each other, and I've been in restaurants where people with their dates were texting during dinner (not necessarily to each other), or talking on cellphones as though the person with whom he or she was having dinner weren't even there. It seems obvious to me that this is not being "connected." In fact, it is being separated, distanced, and disengaged in such subtle ways that many people haven't even noticed how utterly outrageous such scenes can really be.

At the dealership where I had my car serviced this morning I was reading my Kindle to pass the time. Others in the same waiting room were on cellphones, texting, or playing games on their phones. We were all like electronic mannequins in a big box, wired to be activated by the push of some remote button. There was no conversation or interaction among us. I was a guilty as everyone else. The most human among us was a man who was snoring wile fast asleep in a corner chair. I used to feel free to look at people to make simple comments or ask questions in public places. Now there is often the fear of interrupting a phone game or texting, even though the message often turns out to be nothing more than, "Hey...what's up? Nothing here."

Maybe as we become more crowded on our planet, especially in public gathering places, we begin to feel more protective of our immediate space. What better means to keep other people away from our physical areas than with cellphones or texting devices? People used to use newspapers similarly on trains and buses to close themselves off, as though in separate paper cubicles to avoid any possible conversation or other invasion of their solitude.

With all our new ways of "communicating" electronically, we are more isolated than ever. I don't know if it's the comforting illusion of being "connected" constantly, or the fear of not being in the network of modernity, but the world to me over the past few years has begun to resemble a kind of science fiction story in which individuals believe that the cure for loneliness is simply an electronic device in one's pocket or purse, the buttons of which will keep everyone from ever feeling quarantined again so that finally, battery chargers will become more important to supporting this grand illusion than human beings themselves.

Chapter 9: Senior Texting

Some wag came up with texting for senior citizens. Most of the elderly people I know don't text anyway, but the humor of these abbreviated messages is amusing without being completely disconnected from fact:

ATD: At the Doctor's

BFF: Best friend fell

BTW: Bring the wheelchair

BYOT: Bring your own teeth

FWIW: Forgot where I was

GGPBL: Gotta go...pacemaker battery low

GHA: Got heartburn again

IMHO: Is my hearing aid on?

LMDO: Laughing my dentures out

OMMR: On my massage recliner

OMSG: Oh my! Sorry, gas.

ROFLACGU: Rolling on floor laughing and can't get up

TTYL: Talk to you louder

Chapter 10: Problems with Modern Packaging

It seems that many common products that in the past we bought in stores and opened easily at home now require tool kits, which may include hammers, screw drivers, and possible explosives.

I suppose the changes in all current packaging began with the horrible random murders committed in the early 1980's by the as yet not apprehended psychopath, who tampered with bottles of Tylenol by inserting enough poison to kill innocent people. I can't imagine the twisted rage that would turn someone into that kind of demonic human being, but the mark left by those murders is still evident in almost every consumable product that needs ingesting after manual opening. Everything from aspirin to orange juice requires some kind of dexterous hand maneuver in order to get at the product, let alone actually use it. Some are more annoying than others, like the little plastic circle with a ring handle that opens sealed containers of orange juice, and cartons of soup or broth. I suspect I am not alone in my having broken off the circle pull, so that a sharp knife became necessary in order to get at the contents of whatever product I naively believed was easily accessible. Several canned goods use a similar pull made of metal. The pull has to be bent back and then tugged in just the right way in order to dislodge the can's lid slowly and rather dangerously. Yesterday, as I was trying to open a can of black bean soup, the design of

53

which undoubtedly came from Fort Knox, the lid jammed near the end of my attempt, splattering black beans on the kitchen wall and dark soup on the counter tops and floor. If the tab breaks off before you've opened the container, calling a professional may be your only option, as continued struggles with sharp, partially removed lids from cans may inflict nasty cuts. I speak of this from experience but will say no more about the grislier details of those encounters.

We need to sympathize especially with disabled and elderly people for whom the daunting task of opening even a can of tuna can demand more stamina than they have left. Think of someone suffering from arthritis or rheumatism. Just trying to open a bottle of aspirin or a carton of milk can be discouraging for them. And that reminds me. Has anyone ever really been able to open a carton of dairy cream, not using scissors or other tools, and without tearing the top to shreds? As soon as I see the words, "EASY OPEN," I simply buy the product, no matter what it is. For products like scissors and butane lighters, manufacturers seal them in heavy cardboard and plastic, so that getting at the contents requires scissors or blow torches. Ironic, isn't it?

Plastic "peanuts" are my pet peeve in packaging larger items. In Tennessee last year, I purchased two antique chairs that had to be shipped to my house in Colorado. The huge boxes were stuffed with the plastic peanuts so that when I opened the boxes, the white peanuts gushed out onto the driveway and were carried by the wind like a snow storm all over my neighborhood. The remnants of the peanuts are still there, and probably will be for a couple more geological eras. The chairs themselves were wrapped tightly in many layers of heavy plastic requiring special cutting tools for over an hour before I reached the final contents of the boxes. Counting the time I was chasing plastic peanuts all over Centennial, I spent almost three hours getting to the two chairs inside, which by that time seemed only a dim memory of what I had fallen in love with in Tennessee a month before, due in part to my exhaustion.

The result of all this is a kind of nostalgia I experience in remembering the days when

opening common and necessary products
didn't yet pose challenges more horrific than
those of a Rubik's Cube.

Chapter 11: "Old People"

These points I found on the internet as public domain and worth sharing:

1. Nothing sucks more than that moment during an argument when you realize you're wrong.

2. Sometimes I'll look down at my watch 3 consecutive times and still not know what time it is.

3. I totally take back all those times I didn't want to nap when I was younger.

4. There is great need for a sarcasm font.

5. How the heck are you supposed to fold a fitted sheet?

6. Was learning cursive really necessary?

7. Map Quest or Google Maps really need to

start their directions on # 5. I'm pretty sure I know how to get out of my neighborhood.

8. Obituaries would be a lot more interesting if they told you how the person died.

9. I can't remember the last time I wasn't at least kind of tired.

10. Bad decisions make good stories.

11. You never know when it will strike, but there comes a moment when you know that you just aren't going to do anything productive for the rest of the day.

12. Can we all just agree to ignore whatever comes after Blu-Ray? I don't want to have to restart my collection... again.

13. I'm always slightly terrified when I exit out of Word and it asks me if I want to save

any changes to my ten-page technical report that I swear I did not make any changes to.

14. I keep some people's phone numbers in my phone just so I know not to answer when they call.

15. I think the freezer deserves a light as well.

16. I disagree with Kay Jewelers. I would bet on any given Friday or Saturday night more kisses begin with Miller Light than Kay.

17. I wish Google Maps had an "Avoid Ghetto" routing option.

18. I have a hard time deciphering the fine line between boredom and hunger.

19. How many times is it appropriate to say "What?" before you just nod and smile because you still didn't hear or understand a

word they said?

20. I love the sense of camaraderie when an entire line of cars team up to prevent a jerk from cutting in at the front. Stay strong, brothers and sisters!

21. Shirts get dirty. Underwear gets dirty. Pants? Pants never get dirty, and you can wear them forever.

22. Even under ideal conditions people have trouble locating their car keys in a pocket, finding their cell phone, and Pinning the Tail on the Donkey - but I'd bet everyone can find and push the snooze button from 3 feet away, in about 1.7 seconds, eyes closed, first time, every time.

23. The first testicular guard, the "Cup," was

used in Hockey in 1874 and the first helmet was used in 1974. That means it only took 100 years for men to realize that their brain is also important.

I was in a Starbucks Coffee recently when my stomach started rumbling and I realized that I desperately needed to fart. The place was packed, but the music was really loud so to get relief and reduce embarrassment I timed my farts to the beat of the music. After a couple of songs I started to feel much better. I finished my coffee and noticed that everyone was staring at me. I suddenly remembered that I was listening to my iPod (with ear piece) - and how was your day?

This is what happens when old people start using technology!

Chapter 12: The Odyssey Revisited

From December 6, 2012 until April 27, 2013, I was living in the beautiful Pompano Beach condo that belongs to my partner Jim and me. Jim needs to work one more year before his retirement, so our cat Riggs lives with Jim in our Colorado house, while our dog Dudley and I spend the fall and winter in the Florida condo. I've been retired for ten years, so I'd rather keel over from heart failure playing tennis, bowling, or swimming, than from shoveling snow. Because shipping pets can be dangerous or, at best, traumatic for them, I've opted to drive the 2200 miles to and from the condo for the dog's comfort and my peace of mind. It's about our trip back to Colorado this past week that I'd like to write today.

I've never been a good traveler, probably because I don't "transition" well or very quickly from one location to another, even though I've been to Europe several times. Though I enjoy occasional change and adventure, there is also something to be said for that feeling of being anchored and secure (however illusory the sensation) in just one or two places. In a world that is changing ever faster, the emotional comfort of having a safeguard or mainstay location is gratifying. I'd have made a completely unsatisfactory nomad.

After closing up the condo and leaving a set of keys with a trusted neighbor, Duds and I began the first part of our journey on the southern portion of the Florida Turnpike at around seven that morning of April 27. The first part of the drive was quiet and uneventful, maybe because it was an early Saturday morning, so I was happy with the minimal traffic, even though there were signs from time to time warning drivers of possible delays due to "Spring break" travel.

Duds and I stopped at the Claremont motel in Valdosta, Georgia late that afternoon. The room was comfortable, and there was a good restaurant next door. Drifting off to sleep after watching Rachel Maddow, one of my favorite commentators on MSNBC, I was able to rest until just after two in the morning, when I heard someone pounding on the door two rooms down the hall. The pounding was accompanied by the voice of a man saying loudly, "Aw, come on, baby. Open the door. I'm real sorry, sweetie." Hoping that the woman would open the door to let the man in some time before dawn, I waited as his pleas degenerated over the next ten minutes to screaming epithets, like, "stupid bitch" and "dirty whore," along with the insistent percussion of his fists punching and his feet kicking the woman's door. I heard a door open, but it was that of another room, from which a man's voice yelled, "Hey, keep it down, moron! We're trying to get some sleep here!" At that point, there was some welcome silence either from the woman letting in the maniac, or from his simply having given up and gone away. I couldn't tell which, but it didn't matter. Things were quiet again, and I was able to fall asleep fairly soon. After breakfast, Duds and I checked out, continuing our drive to Antioch, Tennessee, where we checked into a motel called The Knights Inn.

I should have been more aware of what I was in for, when I saw the "lobby" of the inn. The receptionist was behind what was undoubtedly bullet-proof glass. The shabbiness of the carpet, furniture, and art prints brought visions of Irskine Caldwell's Tobacco Road, about Georgia tenant farmers during The Great Depression. However, any fear I experienced about possible danger was diminished by my fatigue and hunger, so that I paid for the one night stay, along with the ten-dollar pet fee and took Duds and the luggage to room 202, right next to the caretaker's room, which had as its window curtain what appeared to be a huge and badly stained tee-shirt from some era long gone. On walking along the second floor catwalk, I saw a discarded wash cloth, a large hair pic comb, and some empty beer cans. Again, exhaustion softened the harsh reality of these giant clues.

Inserting the key card, I opened the door to see the room, and the bed which was nailed to the floor. The smell of the space was that of unmistakable mildew as my eyes were drawn to the upper walls around the room, which at first appeared to have a border of floral design, but which was actually the pattern of mold or mildew recently painted over in order to hide the fact. My only thought was that we could be gone by early morning before any mold could burst through the paint in time to harm us in any way. There was a TV, but there was no coffee maker or shampoo. In the shower was a bar of soap that Barbie and Ken would consider too small, and a bath towel that at home I would probably use to dry dishes. The shower knob had to be turned very carefully to get water, as the knob kept falling off. The general dinginess of the place made me think briefly that it could be a hot property for any producer doing a remake of

Alfred Hitchcock's PSYCHO. This was really the Bates Motel.

I gave Duds his dinner and a dental chew stick to keep him occupied while I dined at the Mexican restaurant next door, which turned out to be a great place to have dinner on a colorful veranda in the shade. I needed the extra margarita to face going back to that dreadful room, but by then, I was too tired to be concerned about anything less than a level five tornado or an army of angry red fire ants.

After I took Dudley for a short walk, I noticed three cars in the parking lot that had trunks and hoods that had been pried open. The scalloped edges spoke of midnight crowbar invasions. Two hoods were wired shut, and one was closed by duct tape. Suddenly, by contrast, my Honda Accord looked like a Rolls Royce, but I had a brief vision of tape and wire holding it together on the remainder of the trip home in the event of a nocturnal vandal or thief. Even all this wasn't enough to keep me from falling asleep almost immediately after I went to bed.

Just after three in the morning I was awakened from a dream about delicious cheese tostadas by loud voices in the parking lot below my window. Pulling the curtains aside slightly, so as not to be seen, I saw an enormous black woman wearing a muumuu the size of a camping tent, arguing with another black woman with a gigantic Afro unlike any others I had seen since the early 1970's. Though I couldn't make out much of what the two were screaming at each other, I did recognize the old standard insults of "Bitch!" and "Cunt!" yelled at ear-shattering volumes, followed by physical punches, hair-pulling, and kicking. The large woman, named Maggie, took off one of her flip-flops and began beating the one named Shaquita over the head with it. They were only a few feet from my car, which was a greater concern to me than Shaquita's head, which was protected by enough frizzed hair to fill a mattress, and could most likely not be penetrated anyway by a heavy shovel, let alone a rubber flip-flop. Then a burly man, even larger than Maggie, entered the fray, trying to calm the two women, who turned on him together, hurling labels, like "Mutha Fucka." After ten minutes of what became a real brawl, a police car arrived, siren blaring and red lights flashing, followed by the two women being hauled away, while the burly man waved goodbye, laughing his way back to his room. By that time, I was wide awake. I mean, after watching people trying to kill each other in a parking lot outside your room, it's a bit tough to get back to sleep.

For breakfast the next morning, I had a couple of Kashi Pumpkin Spice energy bars

with some cold coffee I had left over in a
thermos. All I wanted was to escape! Duds
and I made a quick exit, never to return. I
threw my key card through the little slot of the
bullet-proof glass enclosure around the
frightened looking clerk before Duds and I
were off to Kentucky, through which we drove
pretty much without interest or incident.
Southern Illinois was filled with lovely
scenery, which I didn't know even existed
there. My only mistake was pulling into
MacDonalds for lunch and choosing a Quarter
Pounder, which I will be digesting until
Mothers Day. The drive that day ended in
Missouri at a Ramada Inn which was, by
contrast with the Knights Inn, the Taj Mahal.
I spent a relatively luxurious night there,
sleeping well, and feeling much renewed by

morning. I wondered why the previous place had been named Knights Inn. The only reason I came up with was that the renowned Knights of the Round Table in King Arthur's court had to prove their bravery through tests of endurance during activities, like duels and jousting. Staying at that motel would certainly have earned any Sir Lancelot a place of honor with other knights, who had shown extraordinary courage. In the end, though, were I attempting to demonstrate daring or boldness enough to become a member of the Round Table, I would probably choose jousting or fighting dragons over staying at the Knights' Inn.

Tuesday, April 29th was the fourth day. Duds and I drove through Kansas, which seems to be, at least along Interstate 70 West, one huge fossil with a few twigs growing out of it (not actual living trees). Having heard the blizzard warnings for the plains and Colorado coming Wednesday, I chose to keep driving the extra four hours to arrive home early Tuesday evening. It's a good thing I did. There was indeed a blizzard Wednesday, but my car was already parked safely in the garage by then. Now I'm expecting e-mails from all my friends, who know how much I hate driving. The notes will all be pretty much the same message: "Congratulations, John, for not being killed on your trip home."

Chapter 13: Eluding Molly

I live in a little gated community of condominiums on a small lake in Pompano Beach, Florida. I like my neighbors, but I'm having a problem with one of them, a seventy-five-year-old woman named Molly, who uses a walker to navigate her way around the second floor, where my apartment is.

Molly is a spry lady, despite her dependence upon the walker, and she has the booming voice of a Teamster union rep. She can be heard all over the complex without the benefit of a megaphone, but a bizarre set of circumstances came about to help me realize why people scattered when they heard Molly's less than mellifluous voice coming down the walk. For me, it began when she knocked on my door to ask me to change her air conditioner filter. Then she wanted me to open a jar of pickles, followed by other requests to check this or that in her apartment. I realized finally that there was something terribly amiss, when she knocked on my door to ask me to put a hairnet over her new permanent in order to protect a do for which she had paid fifty dollars. She said that I should not mention to Steve, Harvey, Pearl, Donna, or Marilyn, the other residents on our floor, that I had helped her. When I asked why, Molly's reply was simply, "Oh, they were nasty about it and refused to help." At the time, I took her answer at face value, not putting the puzzle pieces together until later. I simply put the hairnet on her head and continued fixing my lunch. Minutes later there was another knock on the door. "John, my phone isn't working. Can you come over and look at it?" My first thought was, "Do I look like a telephone repairman to you?" but I held back actually saying it aloud. I followed Molly to her apartment, where her cell phone was charging. The illuminated screen read, "Battery charging," so I told her to leave it alone for at least an hour to allow the battery to be strengthened. With no land line phone, she needed the cell. I understood that. I returned to my apartment, where only fifteen minutes later there was another knock at my door to say that her phone wasn't working yet. I sent her back saying that I would go to her place after the hour was up. After the phone was turned on and working again, I believed, perhaps naively, that I had seen the last of

Molly for the day.

Three more knocks on my door were to inform me that her toaster wasn't working, her TV remote was stuck, and that her hair net had come off. The toaster wasn't plugged in, the TV remote batteries were loose, and her hair net had snagged on a coat hanger in her closet. OK, I started to feel that she was simply lonely and looking for any excuse to talk to somebody, anybody. It was, however, after her sixth knock on my door that I became annoyed enough to ponder the circumstances in order to figure out that the real reason she wasn't knocking on the doors of other residents was that she had already done that enough times to annoy them too, so that one by one they told her to go jump off the nearest cliff, with or without her walker. I must have been the only one left who hadn't rebuffed her requests for help. I was apparently still fair game.

Today, there were intermittent knocks all afternoon on my door accompanied by Molly's inimitable voice yelling, "Hey, John. My phone is on the fritz again. What are we going to do about it?" I admit it. I'm a coward in the sense that I don't want to confront Molly with what I would really like to tell her, which would go something like this:

"Look, Molly. I'm not your caregiver, and I don't WANT to be your caregiver. After your sixth knock on my door yesterday, it occurred to me that you were a lady, who uses people, and that you would continue using me as long as I didn't protest. Well, my dear, I'm protesting right now. I don't know what makes you think that these are my problems, and I certainly don't get your sense of extreme entitlement in the matter, but you need to begin solving problems yourself. Your Miss Congeniality trophy is in serious danger of tarnishing. Honey, if you can't even put on your own hairnet, you probably can't make toast or even brush your own teeth and shouldn't be living alone in an apartment. Maybe you need to be in assisted living, a nursing facility, or the hush-hush ward at Imperial Point. You seem to have no sense of borders, limits, or extremes, so I'm telling you now that my door is wired to deliver a high voltage shock if you ever touch the knocker or doorbell again. Do you understand what I'm saying, Molly? Is any of this getting through that hairnet?"

The worst part of all this is that for the past couple of days I've been turning out lights, turning down the sound on the TV or radio whenever I heard the sound of Molly's walker inching its way down the walkway on the second floor, and not answering the door when she knocked or rang the bell. I admit that hiding from a seventy-five-year-old woman is about as cowardly as one can get, but the alternative is being brutally honest with her, which I'm not yet ready to do, but give me a couple more days.

Chapter 14: On Being OCD

I suppose this may turn into some kind of confession, but it would be seen as such only by people who see me on the train, walking down the sidewalk or in a grocery store. Strangers might not guess that I have an obsessive compulsive disorder, and it has nothing whatever to do with being elderly, except perhaps that the inclination has become more focused with age.

My friends and family are well aware of my frenzy for a sense of harmony and order, though I don't impose my mania upon others, except maybe my partner Jim, who doesn't dare leave an unfinished drink on a table for fear of returning a moment later to find the glass washed, dried, and put back into the cabinet, or a clean shirt innocently draped over a chair and being found just seconds later in the dirty clothes hamper upstairs. I don't do these things to aggravate others. My actions are simply automatic responses to what my mind (or what's left of it) sees as parts of my world being in some way out of alignment.

Part of all this nonsense is based upon my excessive desire to be able to find things right away when I need them and not to see them scattered about. An avid fan of the TV show Hoarders, I am repeatedly fascinated by people whose lives seem to have no anchors of material organization and for whom even finding the household vacuum cleaner can mean calling in a team of professionals to do a major search, while wearing masks to avoid the fumes from the pumpkins and grapefruits that have been on the kitchen counter since 2003. Of course, those hoarders might see me as an extraterrestrial creature too, one that organizes linens and pantry items by color. Maybe a TV show about obsessive compulsive folks like me would entertain the crap out of hoarders. Who knows?

A friend told me last week that I was so OCD that I should really be labeled CDO, only because of my inclination to number or alphabetize everything in my home. Though Don was spot on regarding the issue, I was a bit put off by his remark, because I see myself as being politically liberal, generous to friends, family, and worthy outside causes. I would never dream of judging or criticizing organizational habits of friends, even if those habits resembled those of Ma and Pa Kettle.

I admit to being Felix Unger, and I believe that Jim would have to admit being Oscar Madison. I make sure that Jim's wallet never goes through the washing machine cycle, but he solves problems involving plumbing, carpentry, and electricity. He asks me almost hourly where things in the house are, everything from an electric drill to a paperclip, and I invariably know the location. Our two worlds collide in practical ways, as one partner takes care of the other, always defusing anger that for other couples might mean one of them being found eventually buried under a freshly poured concrete driveway.

The advantages to someone living with an OCD person are that there will never be dirty dishes in the sink, that clean laundry will be folded neatly and organized in drawers and on coat hangers, that there will be clean windows, carpets, and floors, and that everything in the house will have its place in an environment of comfortable, physical stability. The downside might be that the Oscar Madisons in these households will feel, by contrast, even more like slobs than they ever did before.

If it were up to Jim to organize the house, it would contain stray shopping carts found on the streets and filled with our worldly possessions. Our tax records and other important documents would undoubtedly be stored in old pizza boxes, possibly by year but more than likely by the dried pizza toppings on the outside of each box.

I shudder to think of the rebuttal Jim might create in response to my little diatribe, but if he writes one, I'll be glad to post it, if only in the interest of sequences, organized communication, and humor itself.

Chapter 15: Remembering JFK and Being Young

 It has been said that every American conscious of events in the autumn of 1963 remembers where he or she was on November 22 of that year. The impact of that afternoon had the power to etch itself forever upon the collective American psyche, perhaps as much as Pearl Harbor on December 7, 1941, or the terrorist attacks of 9/11 in 2001. No one alive at those times can ever forget the percussive shock of those colossal incidents in our history as a nation, incidents that had a way of funneling their way down to our personal lives and personal recollections. I was seventeen years old when JFK was assassinated, and today in his memory and the memory of what we used to be as a country before we lost ourinnocence, I'd like to share what I recall of that time.

The presidential election of 1960 was the first of which I had much awareness. When Eisenhower was elected in the early 1950's, I was only six years old. At home in 1960 my family and I watched the Kennedy/Nixon debates on our black and white television set, and I remember only that something about Richard Nixon didn't ring true to me, because everything he said sounded prepared or even memorized. My Aunt Hazel and Uncle Walter, staunch Republicans, paid me five dollars to wear a Nixon campaign button to school for a whole week, and as a fourteen-year-old, I thought five bucks was a huge amount of money. However, I wore the button to school only once, as it seemed every other kid wearing a button wore one for JFK. When cute Shirley Bodner offered to give me a JFK button, I immediately put the Nixon one into my back pocket in order to fit in better with my peers. None of this had anything to do with actual politics. Once again it was all about image. Jack Kennedy seemed younger, more confident, and more articulate than Richard Nixon, who appeared to represent more of the same old thing from Ike's eight years as President. Change meant some excitement, and to us fourteen-year-olds, that was a good thing. Not wanting to disappoint Aunt Hazel and Uncle Walter by revealing my betrayal of the Republicans, I continued to wear my Nixon button whenever I was around them. Despite feeling two-faced about the whole thing, I never returned the five dollars. That decision was based upon the rationalization that if my aunt and uncle were prepared to bribe a future voter or attempt to buy votes for Nixon, they were as guilty of political graft and corruption as I was of being a freshman hypocrite. As it turned out, I spent all five dollars over a period of two weeks on sodas at the Walgreens on Hohman Avenue in downtown Hammond. Guilt did follow me, however. When Nixon lost the election, I felt personally responsible, as though my not wearing his stupid campaign button had made him lose. Sodas after that election never again tasted as good.

The Kennedys made me feel proud to be an American. Their taste, style, elegance, eloquence, and beauty were lavish in the media, and no one could ever forget January, 1961 on that very sunny but bone-cracking, cold day watching the inaugural speech in black and white and hearing those immortal words, "Ask not what your country can do for you. Ask what you can do for your country." Despite the cold day and the cold war with the Soviet Union, I felt happy that the President and his beautiful and accomplished wife, Jacqueline, represented us on the world stage where, by contrast, Premier and Mrs. Khrushchev looked like Mr. and Mrs. Potato Head. By the spring of 1961 even the Sears catalog had pill-box hats, Chanel-like suits for women, and sheath dresses. Girls at school were already copying Jackie's daytime bouffant hairstyle. The problem was that some girls copied Jackie's evening formal do with hair piled high in elegant but inappropriate swirls that didn't really go with pleated plaid wool skirts the girls wore to school or the white tennis shoes with white anklets. The result over the next two years was that hairdos for girls became quite large, so that some, like Wanda Jenkins and Judy Sabo looked top-heavy, and wearing those tiny bows in front made it look as though the whole giant wad of hair was being held in place by the miniscule piece of ribbon, which might give way at any moment so that all that hair might just give way to fill the room with the ratted thatch.

I also felt proud, because of the Kennedys, to be of Irish descent on my mother's side. Despite Joseph Kennedy's shady, amorous, and business dealings going back to the

1920's, the Kennedy family did become the closest thing America had to royalty. My Irish connection, remote as it may have been, somehow made me and my Irish friends and relatives feel a little closer to Hyannis Port and Martha's Vineyard, and even the White House. I knew nothing yet of Vietnam, and the Cuban Missile Crisis was a year down the road. Life was good.

November 22 that year was a windy day of rain and gray skies in Northwest Indiana. At school that day was another cafeteria lunch of macaroni and cheese with sliced hot dogs thrown in for good measure and a dessert consisting of mammoth cubes of chocolate cake and fudge frosting that must have been leftover rations from World War II. Barney Blue was the only one who actually ate his.

The rest of us left ours on our plates at the tray return window behind which we imagined all that cake being recycled as future desserts or possible building materials to be sold eventually in hardware stores everywhere.

French class with the plain, wiry, but effective Madame Rainey was after lunch. She was an intelligent but very emotional woman who gave everything to her teaching, always assigning and later grading carefully the huge amounts of homework, expecting all of us to be consistently prepared, based upon work she had given to us. She would walk up and down the aisles between rows of desks in order to stand over and gaze at (intimidate) whoever was called upon to respond to her questions. Her nemesis was Jerry Nagdaman whose lackadaisical answer was always, "Je ne sais pas" (I don't know). His total lack of concern for anything we were supposed to be learning in the class seemed to be an enormous blow to Madame's sense of her own worth as a teacher, and twice that semester Jerry had already slumped down in his seat, falling asleep, not waking even at Madame's high volume urging. Both those times she became so distraught and ultimately enraged, that her retinas detached, leaving her temporarily blind, so that Sally Patterson in the front row had to push the intercom call button to summon the school secretary to lead Madame downstairs. The principal would then drive her to the eye clinic. After that for a day or two we would have a substitute teacher whose retinas Jerry could not detach by his annoying inertia. Needless to say, Jerry was not in our French class second semester but rather enrolled somewhat embarrassingly in the only other class with room for him, home economics, where Jerry was the only male, which by all accounts turned out to be more of a reward to him finally than a punishment.

That November 22 as Madame Rainey was talking about French verbs and conditional tenses, the public address system came on. We had all heard the drone of announcements so often during any given day that they generally drifted through our somewhat empty heads like air through whistles. Mr. Witham, our school principal, repeated the words so that more of us tuned in to what he was saying. "The President has been shot in Dallas, Texas." The numbing, if slow-moving effect of that sentence created silence in that room, broken only by the next announcement just moments later, "The President is dead." Madame Rainey had to lean back on her desk top, putting her hands over her face in a useless attempt to hide her tears. As though on some kind of electrical circuit, sobs began to move through the rows of students, especially girls, some of whom were weeping openly, others simply crying, "No, No, it can't be true." Walter Cronkite's announcement played again on television that evening as he removed his glasses to wipe away tears, would be repeated many times over the next few days and help to bind us as a nation into a kind of shared grief seen through TV news coverage of so many sad faces of young and old alike. Images of the young widow, Jacqueline Kennedy and her two children would continue to haunt the entire country and the world for decades to come. We would all come to look back on that time as the day we lost our innocence as a nation and as a generation.

I can still hear Samuel Barber's "Adagio for Strings" played many times over the days after JFK's death and how its deep melancholy summoned all that shared grief on a personal level in my remembering someone I had never met but of whom I somehow felt proud and someone whose very house I had visited on our senior class trip to Washington just a month before.

Chapter 16: Driving in Southern Florida

I love Southern Florida for many reasons, including the balmy winter weather, the beauty of flora and fauna, the ocean breezes, the friendly people, and the absence of state income tax. Among those reasons, driving will not be found. Native drivers here continue to astonish me with their apparent oblivion over simple rules of the road that are encountered in most other parts of the country, except perhaps for New York City.

I was here in Pompano Beach for several weeks last year before encountering another driver who used a turn signal. That event was a relief to me just when I was beginning to believe that using turn signals down here might actually be against the law. Strange as it may seem, I thought there could be a different rule in this part of the country...something like, "If you use your turn signal you WILL be arrested and do prison time."

Countless times I have been cut off by other drivers, who simply assume that my psychic powers will notify me that they are changing lanes. In a moment of wild mental abandon, I also wondered if there might be clinics down here, where drivers had those tiny portions of their brains dealing with turn signals surgically removed. Standing in lines at the bank and at super markets, I've been looking at the backs of people's heads for cranial scars as proof that my bizarre notion might be factual. No luck yet in detecting scars like those, despite the bald head of a shopper in front of me at Publix Super Market the other day, a head sporting tattoos of two arrows, one pointing right and the other pointing left. I groped for an interpretation but was afraid to ask what the arrows meant. Maybe he was just bisexual.

In Southern Florida there are also more licensed drivers over the age of one hundred than in any other place in the country. The other day I saw a woman driver I'm guessing was at least two hundred years old, whom I couldn't even see until I passed her vehicle that appeared to be driving itself. She was too short to be detected except for two arms upward grasping the steering wheel. I suppose she wasn't even able to reach the turn signal controls.

Because it is perpetually summer here, many

drivers leave their car windows down and instead of using the standard turn signal lights, those motorists simply lean their left arms out the driver's side in a lazy, casual attempt to let others know of some kind of turn. This attempt, of course is not effective, because such drivers rarely, if ever, form an "L" to show the intention to turn right or use the arm straight out to signal a left turn. It's almost a challenge that says, "OK, everybody. I'm about to do something here with my car. See if you can guess what it is in time not to create a crash."

I continue to use my turn signals from years of not having driven my car any other way and am pretty sure that Floridian drivers behind me see me as an anomaly or simply as someone, who has indulged in fancy accessories for my automobile.

Chapter 17: One Retirement Story

I ran across this vignette written by an anonymous Floridian about his retirement and found it both amusing and instructive:

A Few years ago, my wife and I moved into a retirement development on Florida's southeast coast. We are living in the "Delray/Boca/Boynton Golf, Spa, Bath and Tennis Club on Lake Fake-a-Hachee". There are 3,000 lakes in Florida; only three are real.

Our biggest retirement concern was time management. What were we going to do all day? Let me assure you, passing the time is not a problem. Our days are eaten up by simple, daily activities. Just getting out of our car takes 15 minutes. Trying to find where we parked takes 20 minutes. It takes a half-hour in the check-out line in Wal-Mart, and 1 hour to return the item the next day.

Let me take you through a typical day: We get up at 5:00 am, have a quick breakfast and join the early morning Walk-and-Fart Club. There are about 30 of us, and rain or shine, we walk around the streets, all talking at once. Every development has some late risers who stay in bed until 6:00 am. After a nimble walk, avoiding irate drivers out to make us road kill, we go back home, shower and change for the next activity.

My wife goes directly to the pool for her underwater Pilates class, followed by gasping for breath and CPR. I put on my 'Ask me about my Grandchildren' T-shirt, my plaid mid-calf shorts, my black socks and sandals and go to the clubhouse lobby for a nice nap.

Before we know it, it's time for lunch. We go to Costco to partake of the many tasty samples dispensed by ladies in white hair nets. All free! After a filling lunch, if we don't have any doctor appointments, we might go to the flea market to see if any new white belts have come in or to buy a Rolex watch for $2.00.

We're usually back home by 2:00 pm to get ready for dinner. People start lining up for the early bird about 3:00 pm, but we get there by 3:45 because we're late eaters. The dinners are very popular because of the large portions they serve. We can take home enough food for the next day's lunch and dinner, including extra bread, crackers, packets of mustard, relish, ketchup and Splenda, along with mints.

At 5:30 pm we're home, ready to watch the 6 o'clock news. By 6:30 pm we're fast asleep. Then we get up and make five or six trips to the bathroom during the night, and it's time to get up and start a new day all over again.

Doctor-related activities eat up most of our retirement time. I enjoy reading old magazines in sub-zero temperatures in the waiting room, so I don't mind. Calling for test results also helps the days fly by. It takes at least a half-hour just getting through the doctor's phone menu. Then there's the hold time until we're connected to the right party. Sometimes they forget we're holding, and the whole office goes off to lunch.

Should we find we still have time on our

hands, volunteering provides a rewarding opportunity to help the less fortunate. Florida has the largest concentration of seniors under five feet and they need our help. I myself am a volunteer for 'The Vertically Challenged Over 80.' I coach their basketball team, The Arthritic Avengers. The hoop is only 4-1/2 feet from the floor. You should see the look of confidence on their faces when they make a slam dunk.

Food shopping is a problem for short seniors, or 'bottom feeders' as we call them, because they can't reach the items on the upper shelves. There are many foods they've never tasted. After shopping, most seniors can't remember where they parked their cars and wander the parking lot for hours while their food defrosts.

Lastly, it's important to choose a development with an impressive name. Italian names are very popular in Florida. They convey world travelers, uppity sophistication and wealth. Where would you rather live: Murray's Condos or the Lakes of Venice? There's no difference -- they're both owned by Murray, who happens to be a really cheap jerk.

I hope this material has been of help to you future retirees. If I can be of any further assistance, please look me up when you're in Florida. I live in the Leaning Condos of Pisa in Boynton Beach .

PS. This is printed large on purpose so you can read it.

Chapter 18: Sound Memories

The music we listen to often provides signposts for the events of our lives. A song or other piece of music can be a sensory trigger catapulting us back to moments we think we've forgotten.

Marcel Proust believed, and demonstrated in his monumental novel, La Recherche du Temps Perdu (Remembrance of Things Past) that olfactory stimuli (primarily taste and smell) were indelible sources of recollection. The mere taste of a madeleine (type of French lemon cookie) dipped into a cup of hot mint tea resurrected with great intensity a moment from his childhood thirty years before. Our sensory experiences are often stronger than our intellectual ones in terms of their ability to remain dormant but powerful. The same sensory principle applies, I think, to audio stimuli, particularly ones involving music and human voices. I have a cassette tape my sister Connie Lynn and I made in 1978 of our grandparents. The recording is ninety minutes of conversation with Grandma and Grandpa along with their verbally animated stories of times gone by. Whenever I play it, those voices from all those years ago transport me back to my childhood and youth, despite the deaths of both grandparents before 1995 and the death of my sister in 2011. The timbre of those voices in some chilling, powerful, but unexplainable way, makes me young again just for a moment.

The song, "My Country 'Tis of Thee" takes me back to the fourth grade in the rickety, old portable buildings of Harding School in the early 1950's. Even just the tune to "Happy Birthday" summons scenes of my family gathered 'round cakes with candles to be blown out while making wishes. "Silent Night" and other carols take me back to the Christmas seasons throughout my life and those cold winter nights when the songs had such profound meaning. The Beatles, Peter, Paul, and Mary, Blood, Sweat, and Tears, The Doobie Brothers, Tony Bennett, The Supremes, Judy Collins, and The Temptations carry me back, as if in a time machine, to the dorms of my college days. Whenever I hear "The Adagio for Strings" by Samuel Barber, I experience again with perfect clarity the aftermath and television news coverage of President John F. Kennedy's assassination in

November of 1963.

The ear recalls so much joy and sadness through music we've loved and the voices of those people who influenced us most, especially those from childhood. It's possible for most of us to unearth strong memories tied to associations between music and vivid times in our lives that the music represents. Each of us can create his or her own list of music and voices from the past through sensory and emotional association.

What pieces of music have the most power to take you back to another time in your life?

Chapter 19: Sweet Lorraine

Recently on the evening news there was an item about a man named Fred, who at the age of ninety-six was writing a song about his departed wife Lorraine, to whom he had been married for seventy-three years. Though Fred doesn't sing or play an instrument, he found some musicians, who used his lyrics to create a recording as a tribute. The song is called "Sweet Lorraine" and has been put on YouTube with photos of Fred and Lorraine through the years.

The touching narrative of these two people, so devoted to each other for all those years, is not a new story, but is no less powerful when I think of it in terms of others I've known who were together for most of their lives before suffering the loss of a partner through his or her death. The most recent personal example for me was the death of my Uncle John, whose surviving wife is one of my mother's younger sisters. My Aunt Connie and Uncle John were married for sixty-three years in a loving relationship that was almost symbiotic in the way the two depended one upon the other. Their lives were so intertwined through music, values, and being the patriarch and matriarch of a large family of grown children, grandchildren, and great grandchildren, that John's death created a kind of void, that my aunt is trying desperately to overcome. Her husband's absence continues to be so potent a force that my aunt can sometimes hardly accept the fact that John is gone. She even forgets occasionally and picks up the phone to call him at the hospital.

I can only begin to imagine the remnants of their life together crowding in upon my aunt on a daily basis, sometimes bringing with them tears of joy, and other times bringing a crushing sense of grief. Sleeping next to his pillow, playing old recordings of his voice speaking or singing songs they had so often sung together, seeing his clothes still hanging in the closet, smelling his aftershave lotion lingering in the air, and seeing photographs everywhere of their life together since before 1950. These things make me wonder how many widows and widowers must be in emotional distress through grief the rest of us can hardly realize. In physical terms, such grief must be like having one's legs or arms removed so that life would feel so restricted, that even the motivation to breathe would be impaired.

I remember too, my maternal grandfather's death in 1985, and the photos of my grandmother afterward, her face having lost forever the vitality and gaiety it had always shown before she lost the dearest person in her life. So many are never the same again after such a terrible loss. There is even a physical transformation.

Anyone, who knows a man or woman whose life partner has recently been taken, should have a deep sympathy and a readiness to be available to help the survivor get through this toughest of emotional perplexities that life can present to the human psyche.

Chapter 20: TV Drug Commercials

Use Pylorexene with caution. Side effects may include nausea, internal bleeding, blindness, stroke, desire to commit suicide or murder, uncontrollable urges to stick your finger into an electric light socket, to pee on a neighbor's new car, or to shoplift tubes of expensive toothpastes. See your doctor if side effects persist, and eat plenty of peanut butter.

Of course, I've created an ad exaggerating characteristics of ones I've actually watched on television commercials for pharmaceutical products. There are drug commercials on TV every few minutes, and they have in many cases become so subtle, that I can no longer even identify for what treatments they're intended. The happy faces of the "patients," who are hiking through lovely woodland settings with their dogs, fishing with their grandchildren, or just sitting blissfully on benches in beautiful gardens of public parks, beguile me into forgetting the purposes of the messages, the side effects of the medications often being ultimately worse than those of the ailments being treated with the medications in the first place. It seems that in our modern culture, there's a pill for everything.

Chapter 21: The Gift of Reading

As someone who taught high school English for thirty-five years, I know the value of reading and the joy or sorrow it can bring to students of all reading levels. Old age often brings time for reading we never had when we were younger.

My first motivation to read came from my parents. When I was only two years old, they began a ritual of reading to me at bedtime, taking turns each night. This habit made bedtime a pleasure for me and then for my younger brother and sister. Bedtime stories read aloud became things we looked forward to and provided a peaceful bond between us and our parents. After I reached the age of two, Mom and Dad took us to the public library, where we were able to choose books in the children's section. At that early age, I began by picking books for the pictures and then for the stories. Next my parents would ask us to tell the stories based upon what we remembered of the books, often using illustrations as guides. Then came the words we began to recognize and repeat.

Dad said that if we liked books, we need never be bored or feel lonely. That wisdom was proven true over and over again as I was growing up and is still as accurate as it ever was when I was a child. On every summer trip we took with us in our station wagon a selection of books to read en route. I will always be grateful to my parents for hooking me and my siblings on reading. A new book to read was the one thing we were never denied as kids. There might not always have been money for new bikes, but there was always money for new things to read. My brother David, my sister Connie Lynn, and I could often be found curled up in a cozy corner with books we loved. Winnie the Pooh, The Wind in the Willows, Charlotte's Web, Dr. Seuss, Rudyard Kipling, Robert Louis Stevenson, and Aesop's Fables were among these.

My grandparents bought us the Young Folks Shelf of Books, a set of ten volumes published in the 1940's by Collier. There were earlier and later editions of these books, but I still have the ones given to us when I was still in diapers.

When I taught high school, I tried hard to find books that interested each kid, even though we also had a roster of books in the required reading curriculum. I knew that once a kid found a book he or she loved, a life could be changed forever.

It saddens me at times to see kids constantly using their thumbs to text mind-numbing and uncreative messages instead of challenging themselves with good books. I was delighted by the Harry Potter revolution. I still love seeing teenagers and younger kids carrying books that are their own choices, books that enrich as well as entertain. We can all be sensitized and made better by reading. It's a private joy but also one that can be shared in our discussions of why we liked what we have read as we pass on books to friends and relatives. It doesn't matter if the book is old with yellow pages that smell of the distant past or electronic Kindle Readers. Reading is a window to enhance our curiosity and sense of wonder about everything around us. I urge all the parents out there to make reading a pleasure you share with your kids and grandkids. They will be forever enriched by it and grateful for your loving efforts.

Chapter 22: Tattoos and Body Piercings

I know that body tattoos have been around for hundreds or perhaps even thousands of years and that they are part of what we in the modern world like haughtily to call "primitive" decoration. There are, in fact, elderly people who have new tattoos and other elderly folks who have had them for decades.

When I was growing up in Northwest Indiana in the 1950's, the only guys who had tattoos were the ones who had served in the United States Navy or were members of motor cycle gangs. Our next-door neighbor, Mr. M had a tattoo on his left arm that was an elaborate depiction of the girl with whom he had fallen in love during the late 1930's but with whom he never ultimately even had a date. In those days, there was no such thing as laser removal of tattoos the messages of which turned out to be temporary. The images remained, for better or worse.

Now tattoos are quite common. Many, perhaps most, are small insignias placed tastefully in areas that are not always on display but intended to be shared only with intimates. Less common are the very large and obvious tattoos that cover foreheads, faces, necks, hands, backs, legs, and everything in between and make me think the circus is in town. These are the people, who want or need to advertise that they are in love with someone, hate someone, hate the world in general, or simply crave attention. In the same category, at least in my thinking, are the steel inserts, not just in ears, but also in tongues, lips, eyebrows, noses, and anywhere else that might make an electrical storm more exciting.

Steel inserts can be removed or relocated without too much trouble, but tattoos require expensive laser treatments, when removal is even possible. It's supposedly a free country when it comes to such things, but I continue to wonder why such dramatic gestures are chosen in such relatively permanent ways. The more bizarre or arresting the tattoos, the more likely it seems the wearers would tire of them. It's like buying a suit of clothes in one's twenties so that the same outfit can be worn into old age. Maybe the tastes of some people remain static, as though their identities are incapable of development over the years. It's probably true that what we wear and how we cut our hair say something about who we are, at least at the moment. I like the idea that I don't have to wear swim trunks all the time, or a suit all the time either. I appreciate change the choice I have to blend in different ways according to where I am. I wouldn't dream of wearing now the outfits I wore in the 1970's. How static that would be. I'd feel trapped...but isn't that what someone does with a permanent tattoo, especially one that screams out its message?

I'm guessing that someone in his or her twenties, who chooses a huge and extreme tattoo is unlikely to see it the same way in his or her fifties, sixties, or seventies, when skin wrinkles and sags to alter the previous effects of images previously thought "cool." See a young lady whose neck tattoo looks more like a cancer skin graft.

There are many ways to say who we are through our appearance, but often those ways develop and change as we mature. It's regrettable that what we wanted to be permanent at age twenty might become a liability and sideshow joke at age sixty when it comes to tattoos or metal hardware that make us believe that we may be loved, admired, or just noticed more than if we don't use neon light methods, methods that may prove sadly to be very short lived. I wonder how many elaborately tattooed people wake up one morning, look into the mirror and say, "Oh, my God! What was I thinking?" Imagine a woman with more than the usual number of decorations from tattoos and metal inserts.

This to me represents much too great a commitment, especially one that is devoted to no more than personal vanity.

Chapter 23: World War II Letters: THE IMPORTANCE OF SHARED PERSONAL HISTORIES

I'm not sure at what point one's personal history becomes part of the broader spectrum of human experience. It may sometimes make a connection from the origin of that history. Archeologists rejoice when they find a broken clay jar that once contained olive oil or wine thousands of years ago, or some edict written by hand on vellum affecting lives of thousands under an antique monarch. Certainly, a piece of history like Charles Lindberg's plane, The Spirit of St. Louis, at the Smithsonian in Washington brings more chills to the public because of its great significance in the history of man's attempts to fly. Something already famous, like King Tut's sarcophagus covered

134

with shimmering gold will bring shivers to most viewers. It's something most of us knew about before even seeing it, so it becomes a kind of shared history when we talk to others, who have also seen it.

When I found the boxes of letters written by my father during WWII, I struggled about whether those personal communications would have much significance to the general public, especially those who were not alive during those years 1941-1945. I decided that the backdrop of World War II would be inclusive of pop culture, including music and poster art. It would include many references to a time that was surely our finest hour, when we as a nation were together in a cause of world importance against a powerful evil that might otherwise actually have swallowed up the world had it not been for our collective resolution and united with other nations to take a stand. In that light, every letter home from every soldier in every corner of that massive conflict must surely have significance.

We were fighting for home and for everything we held dear along with the English, the French, the Belgians, and the Dutch, whose lives had also been plundered by Nazis, Fascists, and the Empire of Japan. I don't know that soldiers thought of the grand picture of world peace during the many parts they played in that war. I believe that the things that kept them going were not just the eloquent speeches by Churchill and Roosevelt, but rather the memories of sweethearts left at home, babies on the way, sitting down to Sunday dinners with family, going to the movies or soda fountains, watching ball games. That yearning to return home is as old as history itself and always manages to give a human face to incidents on the world stage, maybe especially in times of war.

Yes, the letters our soldiers wrote home still have a universal connection to what makes us all human. My greatest hope in creating this part of the book was that others who read it would have "eureka" moments too about their own parents, grandparents, aunts, uncles, cousins, sisters, brothers, from that or any other time and wish to honor those people in whatever way possible. So, if you have old boxes of letters, trunks in the attic, family photo albums, please sit down one afternoon and look through those mementos of your own history, and you will discover that what you find there is part of all our history, human history, all that experience that we share as a mortal species through every picture of smiling loved ones in front of Christmas trees or over birthday cakes. Laugh, cry, write about your sentiments, and perhaps decide what you would like to leave behind for others to find seventy years from now as a reminder that you were once here too.

Chapter 24: Saying Goodbye to a Beloved Pet...

A dear friend recently said goodbye to her dog Bubba. My friend and her husband kept a vigil hour after hour during Bubba's final time in this world. I know how difficult it is to lose a pet. Since childhood, I've lost many, and the anguish of that loss is almost unbearable. Here is something I wrote after my dog Cody died in July of 2009. The hope came from getting another dog as soon as possible to help relieve the terrible sense of loneliness:

Cody

In front of me is a small oak box. It sits on the piano and holds the ashes of Cody, the West Highland White Terrier I had for almost fifteen years. How strange that all that love, merriment, mischief, and courage from those wonderful years could be reduced to the meager contents of this little container. It is a feeling of astonishment shared by so many others who have lost ones they loved and who have wept over boxes and urns that held the final physical remnants of who was adored.

But the corporal remains provide only a kind of closure that creates the illusion that physical presence was the only thing. The box is no real comfort, except to remind me of the concrete reality of Cody's existence. He really WAS. His spirit, however, remains in the countless reminders of his still unfamiliar absence. It remains in his favorite tartan plaid blanket, his food and water dishes decorated with tiny paw prints, in his favorite chair, on the brick path in the garden where he loved to sun himself and play.

His spirit resides even now in the barking of other neighborhood dogs, in the white fur that is left in his brush, in his collar, and on the leather leash that made him leap with excitement, even into old age, at the thought of a happy stroll with me. It is in the nose prints on the inside of my car windows, summoning again his insatiable energy, curiosity, and love of everything and everybody around. All that innocence, trust, fun and unconditional love can never be contained by a box of any size. It is all too boundless, and it is a part of me now and for however many years I have yet to live in this world. If there is a veil through which we pass into some other realm, I know that Cody will be there. Then whatever heaven there may be can be complete through the shared experience of his utter joy and mine.

Events after Cody's death made me see something remarkable in the healing process (which continues). I contacted Cody's breeder in Iowa to let her know of his passing, as she and I have kept in contact over the years. I asked if there might be any litters of Westies coming up. Her reply came as a huge but happy surprise, that she was going to retire from breeding and showing West Highland White Terriers but that there was indeed a recent litter with four pups. Three were spoken for, but there was one male left, which several people wanted. She said she didn't know why she had hesitated to sell the dog to anyone yet, despite several requests. The pups were born the very day Cody died (July 17, 2009), and the father's name is Cody II . Can you believe how fortunate I was in this perfect timing? And what are the odds for these things falling together so well at just the right time? I bought the puppy and named him Dudley after an angel played by Cary Grant in the 1947 film THE BISHOP'S WIFE, one of my favorite movies.

Dudley was not ready to travel to Colorado from Iowa until late September, as he was at the time only three weeks old. Jim drove me there to bring Duds home. I was so grateful that all this happened. It was almost as though Cody's spirit had somehow been involved and perhaps even resided in that puppy that I was meant to have. My priority continues to be accepting and nurturing of Dudley's personality and traits without comparing him with Cody (a very tough act to follow).

People sometimes feel a strange kind of guilt at mourning their deceased cats and dogs. I don't know why. Our bond with pets is extremely powerful and fulfilling. The extraordinary and unconditional love we receive in return for meeting their simple needs is surely one of God's greatest gifts in this life. The most important thing, as it is in our bonds with the humans in our lives, is to appreciate and love our pets, giving all the care and attention we can, before the time is up, and we are parted. If you are lucky enough to have a cat or dog, embrace the gift of that wondrous bond in every way you can. Celebrate it every day. If you don't have a pet but are willing and able to love and care for one, there are animal shelters everywhere with loving creatures waiting for your visit and ready to enrich your life beyond what you can even imagine. JB

IF A DOG BE WELL REMEMBERED

 (written by Ben Hur Lampman & published in the Sept. 11, 1925 issue of the Portland Oregonian)

We are thinking now of a dog, whose coat was flame in the sunshine and who, so far as we are aware, never entertained a mean or an unworthy thought. This dog is buried beneath a cherry tree, under four feet of garden loam, and at its proper season the cherry strews petals on the lawn of his grave. Beneath a cherry tree or an apple or any flowering shrub

145

of the garden is an excellent place to bury a good dog. Beneath such trees, such shrubs, he slept in the drowsy summer or gnawed at a flavorous bone or lifted head to challenge some strange intruder. These are good places, in life or in death.

Yet it is small matter. For if a dog be well remembered, if sometimes he leaps through your dreams actual as in life, eyes kindling, laughing, begging, it matters not at all where the dog sleeps. On a hill where the wind is unrebuked and the trees roaring, or beside a stream he knew in puppyhood, or somewhere in the flatness of a pastureland where most exhilarating cattle graze. It is all one to the dog, and all one to you, and nothing is gained and nothing is lost — if memory lives. But there is one best place to bury a dog. If you bury him in this spot, he will come to you when you call — come to you over the grim, dim frontiers of death, and down the well-remembered path, and to your side again. And though you call a dozen living dogs to heel they shall not growl at him, nor resent his coming, for he belongs there. People may scoff at you, who see no lightest blade of grass bent by his footfall, who hear no whimper, people who may never really have had a dog. Smile at them, for you shall know something that is hidden from them, and which is well worth knowing.

The one best place to bury a dog is in the heart of his master.

Chapter 25: Our Political Climate

I often wonder how truly accurate or savvy any of us can be about issues flying around our political arena in the United States. There is no other period in my lifetime when such polarized bastions of social values were aimed at each other from the ramparts of our two principal parties. As a nation we seem to be all at once the envy, target, and laughingstock of the rest of the world. Often I think we seniors are pawns in the political game and placed right in the middle of political battles.

It's interesting to me, for example, to observe the often self-righteous extremes of social and political vitriol between Fox News and MSNBC. There are certainly other forms of media, but these two television networks distill down to their purest forms the convictions of Republicans and Democrats. Tweaking issues and facts by leaving out important details has become an art form on both sides. It reminds of the British cartoon posters displayed during World War I of German soldiers wearing spiked helmets and stabbing infants with swords before holding them up in triumph. Both our political parties are guilty of such unapologetic hyperbole to the point at which it becomes almost comic. There's no better way to get an ally than to make someone angry in a shared cause against a monstrous enemy, real or imagined.

What bothers me most is the blind hatred of one side for the other, often funneling itself down to mere name calling and pure meanness of spirit through altered photographs and other caricatures. There is nothing new about such deliberate exaggeration. That sort of furious rivalry goes back more than two centuries of our political landscape, but such rage can have a powerful effect on our figurative and collective vision of whatever and wherever the truth may be.

I've always been suspicious of people who have no doubts, second thoughts, or reservations about their apparently clear-cut answers to spiritual questions regarding God and our "only" ways of seeking and achieving salvation (whatever that may mean) and eternal bliss. If such a person has no questions or no gray areas of thought, I usually run in the opposite direction. By the same token, if someone is so satisfied that he is completely correct and omniscient about the political arena in this country (especially if he or she foams at the mouth), I know the person is emotionally or sentimentally reduced to a simple and puerile black and white view of whatever the truth may turn out to be.

No matter how staunch a Democrat may be, if he can't examine calmly Republican values and try to see the sense of at least some of them, his grasp on reason is impaired by tunnel vision. This works the other way around as well for Republicans. Members of both political parties wear blinders, whether they are the most naïve and fantasy-prone Democrats or the most rigid, gun-toting Tea Party Republicans. On FaceBook almost daily, I see deliberately isolated and trimmed issues posted, creating false impressions and faulty conclusions among readers, who often express indignation and white-hot anger before knowing all the details, which have been cleverly omitted. The result is unjustified anger, simply because people have not done their homework to see important details that help provide an entire picture. This type of vigilante publicity is only half-information, which can sometimes be worse than total ignorance.

I suppose we need both extremes to arrive at some sane kind of middle ground, where we can look at enough sensible details (dispassionately if need be) from both sides and understand them without having brain aneurisms.

Finally, I would love to see literal boxing matches with the political opponents paired off in this way:

Chris Hayes versus Ted Cruz

Chris Matthews versus Mike Huckabee

Ed Schultz versus Rush Limbaugh

Al Sharpton versus Bill O'Reilly

Rachel Maddow versus Sean Hannity

What a great TV special this would make! The sponsor would be Ovaltine.

Chapter 26: Pockets of People

We live in a world that is fragmented by special interest groups represented by social classes, political parties, religious sects, race, education, gender, age, income, even language. Divisions between groups and factions range from subtle to severe, almost to the point of convulsive, as in cases involving fundamentalist religious zeal, separating fanatics from everyone else, even to the point of genocide and other heinous crimes that under any other circumstances would be considered unspeakable acts of horror, even by the zealots themselves.

As human beings we share a need to belong. Being excluded from groups with which we identify in some way makes us feel separate in negative ways, and our sense of self-worth takes a nosedive from the awful feeling of being left out.

At this time of year, for example, group loyalty to sports teams becomes laser sharp regarding the Olympics and football teams for the Super Bowl. That powerful feeling of being outside the borders of acceptance is especially vigorous on a larger scale at a time when the division between the haves and the have-nots (the one percent versus everybody else) is so pronounced. No matter who we are, we are all strangers somewhere in places we feel we don't belong. The borders we create are often purely artificial, or at least more psychological than physical. Our human tendency to categorize is also what prevents us from seeing our species as one vast but varied human family.

Our insatiable need to create comfort zones socially, economically, politically, and religiously creates at times much more strife than harmony. Such divisions are based also upon our all too human need or desire to be "right," which generally means that somebody has to be "wrong" too.

Even the best informed among us live within walls of some kind of prejudice, especially when we accept without question what has been told to us by those who came before. Ignorance breeds ignorance until we see that as human beings, we are probably more alike than we ever suspected. There was a time when slavery was considered by many to be perfectly all right and was condoned even from pulpits all across our country. It seems we can justify almost anything, at least for a while.

It would be a much more harmonious world if we could remember that everyone has a life story to tell and that all those stories contain elements of pain and joy, despair and hope, ignorance and awareness, fear and courage that, in their purest forms, have not changed so very much over many thousands of years, any more than the human face itself has changed in that time.

Our human tendency to look down our noses at others who are different in some ways is perhaps one of the greatest stumbling blocks impeding enlightenment, and it is a stumbling block that cannot really be removed by technology alone. In that sense, we have a long way to go before we reach any mountain top or promise land.

Chapter 27: A Different America

The other night I watched an old episode of The Andy Griffith Show, which was first aired January 14, 1963. Fans of the series voted that particular episode their favorite, and for good reason.

It's a story about redemption and appreciation of life's simplest but best gifts. The title is Man in a Hurry, a story about a city fellow whose car breaks down in Mayberry en route to an important business meeting in Raleigh. Though the episode is fifty-one years old, it shows a man who has become in our own time a universal character of brusque, impatient, insensitive, and assertive behavior. He can't appreciate the simple tranquility of a rocking chair on the front porch, peeling an apple, or even conversation with other people about anything but business and making money. He has become a classic symbol of break-neck speed in getting nowhere, a man whose blood pressure could probably make him explode at any moment.

However, when confronted by sincere kindness, generosity, and good will from the people of Mayberry, the man changes in a way that still moistens my eyes at every viewing of that episode. At the end of the story, he is a different person, one, who perhaps for the first time since his childhood encounters the value of kindness for its own sake and the sincerity of people of compassion. The power of the story hasn't been dulled by the years but has instead only intensified for us in a time when the world seems to be in love with speed and instant gratification, even over human relationships and charity. The episode lasts only about twenty-five minutes and is well worth seeing again, even if you've seen it many times. It's beautifully done in every way...right to the final moment of the story on the front porch of Andy's house. The video of this program can be seen on YouTube under the title of "Man in a Hurry" for the Andy Griffith Show.

Chapter 28: A Remembrance

Winter Comes: Reflections on Winter Years of Life

My sister, Connie Lynn Bolinger, died May 22, 2011, and I have been going through many things she wrote about caring for our mother during the years 1986 until Mother's death in 2008. I think that many will identify with Connie's emotions at remembering the good and bad times with our mother, watching her slip slowly away into another world that Connie and I were able only infrequently to enter. Remembering the old house, I was touched by the recollection of Mom standing in the doorway on winter mornings even when my brother David and I were in high school until we turned the corner waving to her.

Something my sister wrote I found in one of
the boxes of her papers, and those images
came back to me.

Winter Comes

Mother would always stand at the opened
door of our house in Indiana, and watch me as
I walked to school. Rounding the corner, I
would turn and wave to her. Smiling, she
would wave back, blow a kiss, and signal me to
keep my coat buttoned. When I was seven
years old, it was reassuring to know she would
always be there. Years earlier Mom had defied
all medical odds against her when, at the age
of 32, she had the largest neurofibroma in
Mayo Clinic history removed. Surgery left her
with paralysis and a convulsive disorder. She

was diagnosed as terminal, was given about 18 months to live, and told she would never walk again. Fierce independence, fueled by an unparalleled determination, motivated her to dismiss the surgeon's pessimistic prognosis. She bellowed that she had three children to raise, and dying just was not in her scheduled plans.

With grueling therapy, and otherworldly strength given by God, Mother was able to walk again. Despite severely reduced usage of her right side, she never missed a day cleaning house and preparing meals. She was grateful to be alive, and never ceased thanking God for the provision of His strength in that season of her life. When Dad died in 1986, I knew Mom could not live alone. She came to live with me in Nashville, and thus began my journey of caring for and ministering to her. In 1994, Mother was diagnosed with Chronic Dementia, but it did not rear its ugly head until 1997, when she began to exhibit paranoia and skewed judgment. She would place favorite knick-knacks and family photos in hefty bags and hide them under her bed, behind her dresser – any place that would throw off imagined "intruders" whom she believed were absconding with her treasures. As Mother's symptoms worsened, I realized her needs were beyond what I could provide. The winter of my Mother's life has come, and as of this year, she resides in a nursing facility.

I visit her each evening, engaging her in conversation, and making her feel that what she says still has meaning. Too many times I have witnessed the elderly being invalidated.

People can debate all they want over "personhood theories" and quality of life issues. But, when my mother relives a memory, replete with bright-eyed animation, I remember that she is still there under all her medications – under the tangled mess of invasive brain tentacles, and medical terminologies. Mother still sees me as being seven years old. And every night from her bed she watches me as I leave her room. Each time I round the corner, I turn and wave to her, and she still smiles, saying "You button your coat – it's a cold winter." It is difficult to see her so frail now, for I will always think of Mother as strong and determined in the summer of her life, and carry in my heart tender memories of rounding corners with smiles, waves, and blowing kisses.

God bless you, Mom.

Love, Connie

November, 2007

Chapter 29: My Brother David

In April of 2001 my brother David died of lung
cancer. A man of great insight, sensitivity,
and intelligence, he also possessed a terrific
sense of humor and was always able to
become a child again on Christmas mornings,
on birthdays, the 4th of July, and on the roller
coasters that he loved so much. I still believe
he was a musical genius, not because he was
my sibling, but because he had an
extraordinarily inventive nature that created
complex and brilliant new worlds of sound
from the simple strings of his Humming Bird
acoustic guitar. I still miss him terribly. This
year he would be sixty-five years old and, and
we could have accompanied each other into
old age.

FAREWELL TO A BROTHER

Summer is over,

And I'm walking on the layers of it,

Like geological sediment

Pressed down hard by time.

The self I used to know

Lies deep under layers of memory,

Where wholeness lurks just out of sight,

To be studied (if discovered) and cataloged

For later use, then tested for truth

And redeemed without coupons, commas,

Or dead leaves that cluster 'round its center.

One whom I love lies there too,

Buried among goodbyes of

Tears now hard as granite.

The earth spins on that stick

My third grade teacher called an invisible axis,

And gravity keeps us from being flung

Into outer space,

But inner space is what I mean...

With that moment of farewell,

Never to be removed,

But only built upon,

Irrevocably,

A petrified recollection

Of such density, that it remains embedded

Forever in the deepest parts,

Like some hopeless fossil

In that substratum

Of an early April morning,

Perhaps someday to be found

And polished into something else,

A stone for a ring

Or an agate for a cameo

Over someone's heart.

JB

Chapter 30: Partly Cloudy with Possible Showers

I'm generally a fairly optimistic person, basking in the glow of what I believe is the goodness of most other people and the customary beauty of the world around me. Because I tend to focus on the brighter side of things, I suppose it's possible that my view of the world is impaired from time to time by a naively sunny outlook behind which there are issues I'm not used to observing. This is the point where someone might easily bring out a pair of rose-colored eyeglasses and ask, "Are these yours, John?" In fact, I do feel indignation, even rage, at what goes on (or what doesn't) in Washington, I despair at the suffering of the poor, the indigent, and the children and animals who seem to have no voice of their own. I'm not Pollyanna, and I could never have been an Eagle Scout without a special act of Congress, but I do try to be of use whenever I can. Today was one of those days when my hopefulness about things was bruised by a sequence of minor events that perhaps to other people might have seemed comically inconsequential.

When I started my car this morning, the radio was dead, which meant that I had to entertain myself by repeated singing of the only three songs to which I actually know the lyrics, Moon River (from Breakfast at Tiffany's), There is Nothin' Like a Dame (from South Pacific), and I've Been Workin' on the Railroad from the first record I ever received as a kid, singing it around the house until my parents threatened to put me up for adoption. However, these songs get very old after about fifteen minutes, and even though I know the words to the most famous of all time-passing songs, I've been on too many buses for field trips even to consider singing or even listening to One Hundred Bottles of Beer on the Wall, unless I've drunk a few first, which works only if someone else is driving anyway, so I phoned the Honda dealer to make an appointment for my radio to be checked.

During my haircut this morning my barber pontificated about the Donald Sterling NBA scandal, blaming the whole thing on his "vindictive mistress," who, "set him up." I reduced my take on the issue by saying that both Sterling and his girlfriend were idiots, who probably deserved each other, which seemed to shock Frank, who seems to worship anyone with enough disposable income to spend even a weekend in Atlantic City or Las Vegas. Nothing else I said dissuaded him from his certainty that it was "all the bimbo's fault," even if Sterling had really made the racist remarks he was accused of making. Our tiff didn't seem that serious until I got home and noticed with a hand mirror and the bathroom mirror that my haircut was uneven in back, where the hairline appeared to have been done by a four-year-old child. When I drove back, Frank apologized and changed the line as best he could, with the result that I looked strangely like a mannequin whose painted hairline appeared not to have been quite finished. Nevertheless, Frank refused to recant his defense of Sterling, whom I had called a "moron," much to Frank's dismay. When I got home, it was time for lunch, but I was already feeling sorry for myself and too lazy to prepare a meal, so I grabbed a jar from the pantry, opened it, and got a fork, going next to the den, where I sat watching absentmindedly the first program that popped up when I turned on the TV. Sitting on the sofa, eating Aunt Nellie's Pickled Beets right from the jar and listening to a mindless episode of Gilligan's Island, I began to realize I had to pull myself together to get through the rest of the day. Before turning off the TV, I rolled my eyes at the commercial that promised to deliver catheters discretely to my front door.

Then the phone rang, so I turned off the television, only to discover that the call was a salesman trying to persuade me to take advantage of a "once-in-a-lifetime offer" for discounts at hotels in Hawaii. The guy's enthusiasm was impressive for a while, so energetic and filled with passion that I thought it might really be one of my friends playing a joke. Despite my saying three times that I had no interest in making a commitment to the offer, the man rambled on so poetically that I thought at last he should be playing Hamlet on a stage somewhere instead of doing this phone gig. Finally, not wanting to be overtly rude by hanging up suddenly, I told him that I was allergic to coconuts and pineapple, and that I was deathly afraid of Macadamia nuts. While he continued as though I weren't there, I said, "Thanks anyway" before simply hanging up. I suspect he continued his speech to the end before noticing that he was onstage alone, the audience having left the theater.

Then the doorbell rang, causing my dog Dudley to begin barking. It was my next-door neighbor Mrs. Benson, who wanted to borrow some waxed paper for some maple fudge she was making. When I asked her to come in while I went for the paper, she shrieked, "Oh, my God, John! What happened to your shirt? Did you cut yourself shaving?"

Looking down at my shirt, I saw the large and violent streaks of beet juice that must have made me look like something from the ten o'clock news. Of course, I blamed it all on Aunt Nellie. Mrs. B thanked me for the waxed paper, promising before she left to bring me some of the fudge when it was done. As I closed the door and turned around, Dudley was staring up at me the way dogs often do when they are filled with understanding and deep sympathy for our pathetic behavior. He knew I was having a less-than-stellar day, so he went, as usual, into the den and onto the sofa, where I joined him, and he put his head on my lap, looking up at me as only dogs can, with all the wisdom of the ages, as though he were saying, "Yes, John, Donald Sterling is a big jerk, I don't want to go to Hawaii, and I never really liked that shirt anyway."

Chapter 31: Technology and Human Relations

Once again I return to a theme that haunts me almost daily, the place of technology in people's lives. The strides we've made through electronics have been considerable in making life "easier," or at least faster. Of course, speed means everything to us in the modern world. Everything from fast food to fast vehicles is affected by our desire for expedition and what we think makes life "easier."

As someone who is aging, I'll be the first to applaud things that make life less arduous. I appreciate the electric washing machine and clothes dryer. I enjoy the electric coffee maker (though I still often use the French press for brewing coffee). Automobiles, telephones, television sets, radios, Blue Tooth devices, all continue to amaze and help me in one way or another. My criticism, however, isn't as much with the technology itself, as it is with people, who seem forever to be abusing the very devices that are meant to aid us in our daily lives.

Yesterday morning, Jim and I went for our weekly session of four games of bowling (his scores generally in the 200-plus range, and mine usually around 140). Near the end of our session, a Japanese man arrived with his four lovely children and beautiful wife to bowl in the lane just to our left. Every one of them had his or her own cellphone, and while one member of the family would be bowling, the others remained on their individual phone talking away to God knows whom. There was not one attempt to engage in conversation of any kind one with the other in that family. Not one word was spoken, except on the cellphones. It was another in a series of scenarios that are more and more common. The irony for me remains that in a world where we cling to the illusion of being "connected," we seem to be more distant than ever from one another. Many seem to be desperate to keep in constant contact with someone "out there," as though such contacts render the caller or "callee" no longer alone. This sort of electronic prison keeps many shackled to virtual relationships. FaceBook has a bewildering array of expression hurled moment by moment into cyberspace, but statistics have shown that people are lonelier than ever, despite their being engaged more and more in texting and being on cellphones, which have become almost bionic extension of the bodies of some users.

I'm left with a sense of sadness about such things. I miss handwritten thank-you notes. I miss seeing and hearing kids playing outside instead of their being indoors in front of TV monitors or computer screens. I miss eye contact with people walking down the street, who now have cellphones attached to their ears, no more aware of their surroundings and no more capable of smiling or observing what's around them than the trees and flowers they fail to see. We seem to be on an enormous conveyor belt, hell-bent on getting somewhere as quickly as possible, but I don't know where we're going or why.

183

Chapter 32: The Melancholy Beauty of Autumn

I do believe that we can fall in love with places and seasons. Often we remember places that were summer idylls, or we can recall snowy, winter vistas from holidays gone-by, or the melancholy beauty of autumns. Seasons appeal in different ways to the senses, and we can be carried away by the rich colors of a maple tree turning scarlet or amber. My favorite season is fall, that lovely reminder of the impermanent quality of life for us all.

I remember autumns in New England, and Indiana as being among the most magnificent (like Brown County). I now spend my winters in Pompano Beach, Florida, and even though Colorado has had some terrible flooding in its northern parts the past couple of weeks, I have acquired a deep love of the terrain here with views that are as majestic and breathtaking as any others I have ever seen. Perhaps the reader can remember his own times and places of great beauty, ones that he can summon by closing his eyes to bring them back, if only through yearning recollection. I have come to see that season as the place where I am in my life, a season of "mists and mellow fruitfulness" (Keats). I'm not sure what the winter part will be.

Chapter 33: A Departure

Cadence

Someone will bring tea that steams up ghosts of summer afternoons when arabesques of laughter went spinning through the air.

But now her chair remains, wheels locked in place, and only beads of rain spin in the windy air outside.

A life-line of get well cards pulls her mind back to room 242, Arctic white, except for the shawl her daughter made, soft wool in a gold, like sunlight through closed eyelids.

JB

The phone call came on a very warm afternoon August 12 when streets shimmered with heat, and the only sounds seemed to be the hum of air conditioners and the whir of window fans. There was little traffic, and even sidewalks were deserted, because children were indoors. There was a feeling of muffled, almost soundless time from summer being dropped on us like a warm, moist Turkish towel. Movement was minimal. I sat in my room waving a straw fan at my face and listening to my portable radio playing Dean Martin's rendition of "That's Amore," when Mom appeared in the doorway to say that Grandma B was in the hospital with cancer and not expected to live. This news came as a shock, and only gradually did I begin to make little connections to Grandma's heavy

coughing and pallor the previous spring at
Easter dinner and that Dad had nagged her to
see her doctor, even though she had continued
to make light of her increasing weakness.
Mom's words seemed to float on the air like
feathery dandelion seeds on a quiet breeze,
looking for a place to land and germinate.
When their meaning began to penetrate my
brain, their terrible reality took shape, and I
dropped the fan and turned off the radio.
Mom stood there in the doorway for what
seemed forever, a dish towel held by both her
hands at once, her hair tied back by a yellow
nylon scarf, and perspiration beading on her
forehead. There was no expression on her
face that I was able to read. She too must have
felt stunned.

Later that evening after a dinner none of us

was interested in eating, David, Connie, and I helped Mom clear the table and rinse the dishes before getting ready to go to St. Margaret's Hospital and room 242, the same number as our house on Jay Street. Medical staff were everywhere and seemed to look at us children as interlopers. No one smiled or gave any hint that kids might be welcome there. It made me wonder if other kids before us had vandalized or terrorized the place. The sign reading, "ALL CHILDREN UNDER TWELVE MUST BE ACCOMPANIED BY AN ADULT" made me feel again that we were mere trespassers in a place just for grownups.

Dad went in first, and we followed. Grandma B's other three children were already there with a few grand kids, though some of them had to take turns, as there was a limit to the number of visitors allowed at one time. They were all uncharacteristically silent and obviously very uncomfortable in a place where they knew no more than we did about what it really meant to be in that room or how to behave in ways that would not come across as either too light-hearted or too solemn. There were already three vases of roses, hydrangeas, and daisies giving the room a heavy floral fragrance that clashed only slightly with Grandma's Shalimar perfume and the subtle but disturbing background aromas of chlorine and bedpans. The sun was going down so that light through west windows gave everything and everyone a sort of golden glow. Faces looked reverent like ones in frescoes by

Bellini. For a while only little hiccups of talk erupted, even among the adults but sounded like unenthusiastic speeches by children coached to sound cute or even affectionate. Being in that room was like being in the first act of a play none of us had even read, so that we didn't know our parts and merely fumbled for the right words. Most of us stood, because there weren't enough chairs.

Looking all of her eighty-four years and propped up by two large pillows, Grandma sat smiling as she surveyed the room, mentally taking in who was there and who was not, an IV from her left arm to a catheter bag hanging from a bracket above. Her skin was pallid, her face gaunt, like that of the woman in Grant Wood's painting, "American Gothic." Her gray hair was pulled back and held in place by two tortoise shell combs she had owned since before 1920. Instead of wearing the typical and overly ventilated hospital gown, she had on a pink flannel nightgown covered in a print of lilies of the valley. She wore no make-up, but her nails were still painted with the usual deep red polish, and on her left hand was a turquoise ring given to her many years before by Grandpa before their divorce. I looked at her a long time, trying to imagine what it might be like to be eighty-four. She was the oldest person I knew besides Grandpa B, who was then eighty-eight. Their worlds had not touched for years, and a family veil had been drawn between us kids and any discussion of that divorce. Grandma's voice was weak but determined, as it became clearer to us that she was trying to make us feel as comfortable as possible, despite her being weary. When she coughed, there was each time an awful gurgling sound from her lungs that made Uncle Ralph, Aunt Edna, and Uncle Lou turn away as though they wished not to acknowledge even that such sounds had been made. For the first time, in spite of my father's wearing his sunglasses, I saw tears rolling down his cheeks.

I left the room for a moment and went to the nurse's station, where there was an extra chair. The stern and matronly nurse dressed in a blinding white uniform with what looked like an upside down cupcake cap peered at me over her gold wire glasses from behind the counter and told me I could borrow the chair as long as I returned it before visiting hours ended at eight. There were also nuns in medieval habits with crisp white, pleated wimples glowering at me as I carried the chair, as though I might be stealing it to add to my already vast collection at home of hospital furniture. Taking the chair to room 242, I placed it in what was practically the only space left, right in front of the nightstand, next to Grandma's bed. Then I took her cool, right hand mapped by blue veins and kissed it. Wanting to change the solemn mood, I decided to see if Grandma remembered some of the times we had shared during my childhood.

"Remember when you and Grandpa had the farm with cows and sheep, Grandma?"

"Yes, dear, I do indeed. I taught you to milk your first cow and introduced you to real sheep that were unlike any of those fluffy white creatures in nursery rhymes."

"I loved Peanuts, your dog, who sat in my lap when she was a puppy and later didn't like us kids going anywhere beyond the yard's front gate. I remember the polar bear rug in front of your big fireplace, and the penguin that was a cigarette lighter. I also remember the tamed squirrel who lived in the barn. You used to feed him ice cream. What was his name?"

"Bendy," she smiled.

At that point Grandma drooled through a toothless smile, her upper teeth in a glass on the night table, which made Aunt Edna turn away in apparent disgust or sadness. I couldn't tell which.

"Remember when you used to stay with us kids when Mom and Dad went out some

Saturday nights, and we would watch Creature Features and eat popcorn? After Davy and Connie went to bed one night, you let me taste your glass of wine. Remember, Grandma?"

"Yes, I do remember the wine," she said as her eyes began to droop and her hand squeezed mine once more. She then took a long and labored breath and fell asleep just as her hand slipped from mine, and the nurse came in to say that visiting hours were over. I leaned over to kiss Grandma on the cheek as aunts, uncles, cousins and my parents, brother and sister filed out of the room. The shiny and antiseptic hallways seemed even longer than they had when we had arrived, and our walk back to the car seemed to take hours. The only words I heard as we exited the hospital's front doors were spoken by Uncle Lou, who simply said, "I need a drink." On our drive home, no words were spoken. Mom kept a steady gaze out the front passenger window, Dad drove in silence, and David and Connie stared at the floor from the back seat, where I was watching the city lights blur as we passed them until they looked like the images in kaleidoscopes we as kids had all seen and which had been able in those early years to leave us in a state of complete awe.

For several days we didn't see Grandma until David, Connie, and I took a bus to the hospital. Mom gave us money so we could have lunch at Walgreens. It was now late August, and the cicadas had begun their buzzing on those hot afternoons when hardly anyone was outside. The hard, polished, impersonal interior of the hospital corridors gave a cool shock of relief after the heat of the sidewalks outside. There was on the walls in hallways an occasional grim crucifix or painting of a bleeding heart wrapped in thorns, and the floors were highly polished composite stone, like those at school. We took an elevator that whispered quietly up to the second floor and walked silently past rooms that yielded only quick glimpses of mostly elderly patients in wheelchairs, beds with IV's, a man on crutches, and a blue-haired woman being given her pills by a nurse. The only sounds were those of coughing, an old man insisting he be given a cigarette, and a rather loud TV airing "The Price Is Right," Bill Cullen's voice churning up more enthusiasm from an already wildly excited audience. Another nun stopped us, her rosary beads rattling, to demand our visitors' passes. Then suddenly, her granite features melted into something like a compassionate smile before she continued floating down the hall, her long black skirt sweeping the cold floor as she went.

A nurse met us at the door to Grandma's room and explained to us that our grandmother was asleep but that we could stay awhile if we were very quiet. The previous week I had heard a doctor telling Mom and Dad that the cancer had already reached vital organs and that nothing further could be done, except to keep Mrs. Bolinger as pain-free and comfortable as possible. There was a strong smell of rubbing alcohol and peppermint, with the faintest hint of vomit. On Grandma's nightstand were some wads of tissue, a pack of Beeman's chewing gum, and a tabloid paper with a cover story about flying saucers and space aliens. We then drew chairs up To Grandma's bed. The shades were down, and there remained from the previous week only one vase of fading daisies. I took Grandma's right hand in mine once again. Her hand was even colder than before. Her left arm still had the IV. David and Connie looked at the floor, where Grandma's fuzzy pink slippers were near the foot of the bed, slippers about which we had joked so many times during her visits to our house.

While holding Grandma's hand for what seemed like days, I recalled the old tire swing that had hung for many years from the huge oak tree in her back yard and how we kids would spin and fly through the air until we were intoxicated by the thrill of it. I remembered too being three years old and being so fascinated by the sound of toilets, that I dropped Grandma's pearl necklace into the bowl one day just to watch it whirl out of sight and to hear the gush of swirling water. I remembered her fox stole, the magnifying glass she had given me for my sixth birthday, and the accordion she had bought me with such high hopes that I would become another Myron Floren. She had always made Rice Crispy Treats for us when she came to visit and had never been too busy to play a game of canasta with us and make us feel grown up. The image of her poodle skirt one Halloween came back to me and the pink pop beads she had worn to put her gray hair into a pony tail. Then there was the recollection of all those silly super market tabloid gossip sheets that she had accumulated and that had entertained her so.

After more than an hour, I looked at the clock and noticed Grandma's breath becoming suddenly labored and coming in quick little spurts. I told David to find a nurse, but as soon as he left the room, Grandma heaved one long breath, exhaling it into silence. The pulse of which I had been only subconsciously aware had stopped. My saying, "Grandma, wake up!" startled my sister, who stood up and touched Grandma's other arm. There was an awful absence of sound before David arrived with a nurse, who checked pulse and breath before turning to us and in only a whisper saying, "I'm so sorry. Your granny is gone now." Then leading us out of the room, the nurse went to the floor desk to call a doctor while we sat in some chairs in the hall. Mom had already been phoned by the hospital by the time David, Connie, and I arrived back home. My response to all that had happened that afternoon was to go right to bed and sleep for ten straight hours. My dreams were of Grandma B, but there was no awareness in them of her death. Aside from the death of my pet turtle Trudy when I was five, Grandma's death was my first experience with such finality. It was not scary, only unyielding, and so definite in the sense that future Christmases, birthdays, and other family gatherings would be emptier, sadder, and lonelier without her. There was a terrible sense of absence and empty internal space that could not be filled.

It was the 1950's, so my father had to argue with the very traditional minister about the need to have a personal and uplifting service for Grandma as she would have wished. Dad won the disagreement, and the only thing I remember now of Grandma B's funeral is that at the conclusion of the service as guests were leaving, there was a record playing Perry Como singing a song called, "For the Good Times."

AUGUST AFTERNOON

Thelma wore a shawl and rocked

on the two crescent moons of her chair,

while the cat sprawled out

like an old fur piece in front of the screen door.

Henry lay on the back porch swing,

reading a tabloid from the Piggly-Wiggly:

WOMAN MISTAKES GLUE STICK FOR
DEODORANT-

CAN'T TAKE OFF DRESS FOR TEN DAYS...

The photo said it all.

Billy stayed in his room upstairs with a
mayonnaise jar of fireflies from Sunday night,
their uninspired habitat having drained their
batteries, and on the wall next to the open
window, hung a picture of the family together
in the snow one Christmas, the gray and icy
river behind them contradicting the present,
passionate buzz of cicadas outside.

JB

Chapter 34: Saying Goodbye to a Parent

It was October 20th, one of those cool, crisp evenings that smelled of wood smoke and burning leaves, when pumpkins were on front porches, ready to become jack-o-lanterns in another few days. I had taken a walk, and after grading papers, watched on PBS the next installment of a series called ELIZABETH R, starring Glenda Jackson, about the life of Queen Elizabeth I of England. Going to bed at my regular time of ten o'clock, I had turned off the telephone but was awakened sometime after midnight by the brass knocker on the front door. Through the peephole I was surprised to see a policeman. When I opened the door, he told me that my mother had been trying to phone me and that I should contact her right away, but he wouldn't tell me why. My first attempt to call Mom yielded only a busy signal, but I reached her around 12:45 to hear her weary voice tell me that my father had passed away in his sleep just before midnight and that I should come as soon as possible.

My drive there seemed one of the longest of my life, and by that hour, there was a drizzle of rain that splashed sad messages on my windshield all the way. The porch light was on when I arrived at my parents' house on the other side of town, and my brother David's blue Chevrolet was parked in front. I didn't ring the bell but walked in to see my mother sitting on a sofa in the living room, sobbing, my brother sitting next to her with his arm around her. Mom wasn't wearing her glasses, but she was wiping her eyes with a handkerchief. She stood to give me a long hug, saying nothing yet as my brother then gave me a hug too.

"Shall I brew a pot of tea?" Mom asked.

"Yes, please," I answered, a little surprised at hearing those everyday words as the first ones spoken at a time when we were all three on the verge of going into some kind of shock, but maybe they were actually just the right words, ones that could postpone for a few moments the terrible reality of loss we would be facing together full-force, soon enough.

My dad had suffered a massive heart attack in his sleep and had only one convulsive movement, alerting my mother, who was still awake, reading in bed next to him. Calling 911, Mom felt no pulse and detected no breathing from Dad as she waited for the paramedics, who pronounced him dead just after midnight. The county coroner would be there soon.

I was remembering the last conversation Dad and I had only a week before when, in my parents' garden, I told him to mind his doctor in avoiding salt, alcohol, and cholesterol-laden foods of which Dad was so very fond. While flicking his extinguished cigarette away, Dad said simply, "Aw, doctors. Phooey!" Then he smiled at me in his impish way, as though his dismissive attitude might reduce the seriousness of my request.

My mother had fought a long and difficult battle with Dad about his taking prescribed medications and eating the right foods, while avoiding the bad ones. Mom's becoming a food Nazi was only partly effective in the sense that she couldn't monitor every simple move and decision made by her often obstinate husband, who, when my mother went through the swinging door to the kitchen, would take from his lapel or pocket one of the salt packets he had collected from the fast food places he was forbidden to visit, but which all knew him by name. Then he would put his forefinger to his lips in order to let the rest of us know that we shouldn't tattle on him to our mother, the warden.

Dad also kept a stash of giant milk chocolate bars, the kinds that could be used as building materials instead of bricks. His study was lined with bookshelves and books, the perfect hiding place for those big candy bars, salt packets, and bottles of brandy, none of which were found until after his death. His argument, however, had always been in favor of "quality of life over mere duration." He meant to have it his way, in defiance of any powers that be, which meant Mom and his heart doctor.

David and I entered the bedroom together to see our father lying on his back in the same position in which he had died. His face looked surprisingly restful, as though he were just sleeping. There was no hint of struggle or pain, only a relaxed remembrance of our dad that we would carry with us forever, a down comforter up to his chin, his silver hair shining in the light of the lamp next to the bed, the large pillow cradling his dear head. My brother broke down in my arms, sobbing uncontrollably, so that I led him to a chair. His words were garbled, but I recognized the simple question, "Why?" which he repeated again and again, as though the force of asking it over and over would somehow bring an answer.

He and Dad had been best friends as far back as I could remember, playing their guitars together, going to baseball games and on fishing trips together, and sharing confidences that would be shared with no one else, not even Mom. There was something symbiotic in their similarity and loving partnership as father and son. They were cut from the same cloth, and their relationship was one I had always admired and envied at the same time. Though my mother, sister, and I were loved by Dad and David, my father and brother almost shared the same heart-beat and a psychic bond that transcended anyone's understanding, including their own. I knew that Dad's death was going to be even more horrible for David than for the rest of us. It was as though my brother's vital energy, his own life force, were going to be buried with Dad. The final blow that early morning came when the coroner and his team came and unceremoniously placed our father into a black plastic, zippered sack before carrying him out the front door. David collapsed from the sight, which he likened to our father having been removed in a trash bag. He wept for another forty minutes until there were no tears left, and he fell asleep on the sofa.

The wake at Bocken Funeral Home in Hammond was a continuous crowd, changing from minute to minute from the lines of people all the way down the block, a testimony to how respected and loved Dad was. Mom wore a black dress she had borrowed from one of her sisters, and sunglasses, even though we were indoors, because her eyes were so red from crying. Dad's funeral was even more packed than the wake had been, with wonderful tributes through speeches given by his friends and co-workers. His favorite guitar, an old Martin, was leaning against the casket, and I think that was what touched me more deeply than anything else that morning. I had such powerful and happy memories of Dad sitting alone in his study, playing his guitar with such skill and tenderness all the time I was growing up. That was my dad when he was most joyful and at his best.

The burial was difficult emotionally too, as are most other burials due to that terrible sense of finality, which some may call "closure," when the coffin is lowered into the grave, even if the sun is shining, as it was that day in an azure sky. The head of everyone there was bowed in prayer or at least in respectful silence, but I looked up at the life-size statues of Matthew, Mark, Luke, and John in a semi-circle, where Dad's grave was in the "Garden of the Apostles" at Chapel Lawn in Schererville, Indiana. The granite stone would be for Mom too, her name already carved there with only her date of birth. As the casket was lowered to the point of disappearing, I smiled at remembering that before the funeral at my parents' church, my sister Connie had slipped a giant milk chocolate bar into Dad's open casket, a gesture our dad would have appreciated and applauded.

There was a luncheon at the church after the burial with beautiful food prepared by the ladies of the congregation. Crowds of personal and family friends were there to comfort and energize our spirits as best they could, but for a few minutes my brother, sister and I slipped away to ponder some issues facing us. We half-jokingly decided that because Dad had been only one month from his retirement, the timing was certainly poor on one hand, that he wouldn't be able to enjoy the leisure he so deserved. On the other hand, the timing might have been a blessing in disguise, considering the fact that he and Mom would have been thrown together with no real release valve for Dad to escape Mom's incessant requests to fix screen doors, empty garbage, lift his feet every few minutes so she could vacuum underneath his chair, go to the store for milk or eggs, or wash a second-story window on which she had spied a smudge. No, in those terms, we decided that Dad's exit was perhaps better timed than anyone could really understand. We kidded one another that had he lived, there would probably have been a homicide within six months anyway with Dad as the prime subject of the evening news, and Mom's having achieved the true martyrdom she had always dreamed of.

Though I offered to keep Mom with me in the house I had purchased three years before, she decided to go with my sister to Nashville, Tennessee instead, where my sister had been living and working since 1984. Selling her house and most of its contents very soon after Dad's passing was a sign of Mom's wisdom in deciding not to allow any emotional festering to anchor her forever among mementos of the past, those material reminders of what she and Dad had shared since 1944. Putting her sentiments on hold, Mom started her new life in Tennessee, where she immediately made friends through the church that she and my sister attended. Aside from boxes of family photos, her sweet dog (a terrier named Benji), and items of jewelry Dad had bought for her, Mom let go of most of what could have so easily prevented her retreat into a new life. Taking a deep breath, she moved on with very little looking back.

One week after Dad's funeral, our brother David was in St. Margaret's Hospital with what his doctor told us were "sympathetic heart palpitations," resulting from our father's death and David's profound need to keep some kind of powerful connection, irrational as that might have been. That emotional tie between them was so strong, that in a strange way, my brother wasn't just grieving the loss of our father. He became our father.

I was happy to get back to school, even to the

annoyances and problems of my work there that would help to take my mind away from the pain of grief, which never goes away completely but subsides over time. Teaching school provided reasons to get up early each morning, giving me a sense of purpose through daily goals and projects with a hundred and fifty teenagers, who were somehow keeping me young.

Chapter 35: Aunt Mae

Mae was the sister of my paternal grandfather, and when I was a child, my older cousin Richard's calling her "Great Aunt Mae" confused me into assuming that she was simply a terrific lady. The fact that she was my dad's aunt somehow escaped me. Every time she came to visit, she gave me a crisp new dollar bill, so it was easy for me to think of her as being pretty great. Genealogy, for me, had nothing to do with it. She was a very nice lady who gave me a buck whenever we met.

Aunt Mae had lived in Pennsylvania much of her life, raising two daughters, many of those years as a widow before she moved to Washington, D.C. and worked as a stenographer for the United States Senate. Though she was industrious and energetic, Aunt Mae responded to the shock of Uncle Henry's death in 1951 by never letting go of her sense of fashion from that year. Like so many other women, who have suffered the sudden and tragic losses of husbands, Aunt Mae seems to have put something permanently on pause, perhaps as a kind of anchor that kept her moored safely in that happier time before her husband died. For Mae, her clothing style froze in 1951, never changing at all until her own death in the 1990's. To accomplish this personal suspension of the otherwise unceasing movement and development of fashion, Aunt Mae had to have her clothes made to order, so that even through the 1980's and much of the 1990's she remained a fashion plate from

1951, untouched by time or the changes in women's wear all around her. The Dior-style suits, silk blouses, hats, and shoes, all in the style of 1951, made her stand out in any crowd, partly because she was so statuesque. She always wore her double strand of white pearls too, but it was her tortoise shell glasses that intrigued me most, adding to the very tailored and academic look that made her unique, if not completely eccentric.

Anyone who remains unaffected by clothing fashions for almost fifty years will also have strong opinions, impervious to the many swirls of change and disagreement all around. That was Aunt Mae, a woman of powerful conviction that often spilled into severe judgments on everything from how to brew tea to what the President should be doing (and she would write to let him know from time to time). Also a woman of kind heart, she always meant to be helpful and never thought of herself as interfering in any way, but rather through her healthy ego, she saw herself as the solution to almost any predicament.

Aunt Mae was eighty-seven years old when she wrote to me that she would be paying a visit. The last time I had seen her was when she stayed with Mom for a few days after Dad's death in order to help Mom get through at least the first part of that ordeal. Now that Mom was living with my sister in Tennessee, it would be my guest room that would accommodate dear Aunt Mae for her sojourn away from Washington. Knowing how fastidious she could be, I ironed every pillow case and napkin, and gathered up as many remaining molecules of dust I could find. Over the phone my mother wished me luck, and I could hear my sister Connie laughing in the background saying, "She'll have him standing in a corner after two days."

When I picked up Aunt Mae at O'Hare Air Port in Chicago that windy March afternoon, I was surprised to see that, even at age eighty-seven, she was still as majestic as I remembered from my childhood. She was wearing a tweed suit with black felt beret, like the ones she had worn since before Eisenhower was elected President. After retrieving her luggage, we stopped for tea at one of the air port shops, where Aunt Mae and I caught up on respective news items from the family out east and in Indiana, the sometimes tabloid doings of our remaining relatives, including those of my father's only remaining sibling, Uncle Jesse, who had retired from Inland Steel and started his own lawn mower repair business from his own home.

Aunt Mae expressed her disappointment regarding my brother David, whom she considered a "misguided hippie," only because she hadn't seen him since the early 1970's, when at a family reunion kind of picnic at Wicker Park, David had sported jeans, a psychedelic shirt, long hair, and a beard. It's true that among my very conservative cousins, my brother did stand out, considering that those cousins were the only people I knew who wore neckties to picnics, and I guess the family photo taken of all twenty-seven of us said it all. My brother looked like Jesus Christ on dope among a crowd of others, who appeared to be Baptist missionaries with their wives and children too perfect for me to believe hadn't been rented somewhere for the day. Aunt Mae took a copy of that photo from her purse as we sipped our tea. My assurances that David was a good citizen, fine husband, and terrific father were to no avail until later during Aunt Mae's visit, when I had my brother, his wife, Peggy, and their son Dave over for a dinner during which Aunt Mae's view of my brother softened as she became convinced what a wonderful man he was and how cogent he was in conversation. His not having a bong pipe with him helped too, of course.

Aunt Mae insisted upon visiting my classes at school, where she said she would be perfectly content to sit quietly in the back of the room to observe the "educational process" and compare it to the one she remembered from her own school days. Because I could never deny her anything, it was a done deal. She accompanied me to school for five days of her visit, during which she met the office staff, chatted happily with custodians, and during my conference period even wandered the halls, talking to random students in every locker bay, had lunch with the faculty, learning many of their names, and they hers.

When I introduced her to my Basic English II class, I heard a voice whisper, "Oh, my God! There really is a time machine!" The students were fascinated that my aunt was eighty-seven and that she was taking stairs without even a cane. Considering that most teenagers think thirty is pretty old and that at forty, people should probably be in wheel chairs, Aunt Mae's being eighty-seven absolutely bowled them over and made them quite respectful, even when she corrected their grammar. She

228

was not pleased that some of the students called me, "Mr. B." My explanation that this was done out of a blend of respect and genuine affection did little to assuage her concern that the world was toppling into chaos.

On Friday afternoon she said goodbye to the office staff, who seemed to adore her. Then she walked up the stairs to exchange farewells with three or four other faculty members whose classes she had also observed during that week. As I watched her climb those stairs, I noticed her slowing down just a little toward the top, grasping the railing and wincing, as if in pain. It may have been that she was just sad to be leaving, but I saw her in that moment for the first time as an actual, elderly person, someone for whom all those years had accumulated through her sense of wonder, innocence, determination, and love of people and life itself.

The contrast between her in the old fashioned clothes, and the hard, unyielding stairs of that modern building made her appear to me like a hauntingly beautiful and ancient Gregorian Chant played on some rock radio station, but it was that unfeeling modern backdrop that seemed out of place, not Aunt Mae. As she disappeared down the hallway, I continued to stand at the foot of the stairs, overcome with a sense of pride in this woman, whose life had spread out like a finely patterned carpet over most the 20th Century, a life that had defied the groaning pessimism and fear of growing old by always reaching for the next adventure, the next level in that long corridor with so many doors, all of which she wanted to enter.

Because of her, I would never again fear growing old, if I could only remember my fearless and loving Aunt Mae, who died in 1998 at the age of ninety-three. After her death, Deborah, Mae's only surviving daughter, mailed a package to my mother. It was a little jewelry case containing the double strand of pearls of which Aunt Mae had always been so proud.

Chapter 36: Life in My Condo

My second winter at my Pompano Beach condo in Florida has been even more enjoyable than the first, though soon my dog and I will return to Colorado for the summer.

I continue to enjoy watching (with binoculars) the golfers on the green across the little lake outside my sun room. Part of that entertaining spectacle comes from the varied and sometimes eccentric attire of the players. Some of the more elderly males seem to prefer Bermuda shorts, narrow-brimmed, feathered, straw hats, and wing-tipped black shoes with dark knee socks. No cartoonist could hope to capture the side-splitting humor of this stereotypical clothing, but more entertaining still are the occasional tantrums of golfers, who throw their clubs, or become even more enraged falling into the lake while trying to retrieve errant golf balls before disappearing among the banyans and palms in their little golf carts. Honestly, it's better than anything on cable, with the bonus that voyeurism is absolutely free of charge.

Then there are my neighbors among whom is Molly, two doors down from me. In her late seventies, she is someone who spends most of her time watching TV soap operas and drinking prodigious amounts of wine, which rumor suggests she actually puts instead of milk on her morning corn flakes. Molly had to give up the daily gallon glass jugs of wine she had been purchasing before last fall. The sound of each empty bottle being hurled down the trash chute on our second floor sounded like a bomb going off in the steel receptacle on

233

the first floor. Molly would often choose to dispose of those big glass jugs late at night, perhaps with the flimsy hope that the rest of us would never suspect that she was drinking enough to keep a hockey team permanently drunk. Nevertheless, more than once I peeked out my window blinds after these incidents, believing at first our complex had been invaded by terrorists, but seeing Molly instead wearing her chenille robe and weaving back to her apartment, twice leaving behind one of her pink fuzzy slippers, like some impossible, aging Cinderella on crack.

Another neighbor caught Molly discarding one of those massive jugs one night and awakening the whole building again. The neighbor's only comment to her was, "Molly, if you ever toss one of those jugs down that chute again, I'm seriously going to hurt you."

After that, Molly bought only Franzia boxed wines, ensuring (thanks to the angry neighbor) that the rest of us in the building would get an uninterrupted night of sleep without having to phone 911 to report an alleged, lunatic bomber.

There is a neighbor in the apartment on the first floor just under mine. Mrs. Felding is a widow from Canada who, like me, lives here only during the winter. Her dog is a Boston Terrier with the nastiest disposition I have ever witnessed in a canine. Since Mrs. Felding uses a walker for her mobility, she is unable to walk her fifteen-pound dog, named Cujo (and for good reason). Cujo spits, snarls, barks and lunges at every living creature he encounters. Mrs. Felding's son Warren, who lives elsewhere in Pompano Beach, visits daily to walk the dog at least three times, and my introduction to Warren included a menacing explanation about the terrifying Boston Terrier.

"Be sure never to come near Cujo! Only Mother and I can be around him without danger of bodily harm."

"Thanks for the tip, jackass," I thought. Then I asked myself what could possibly turn a household pet into such a psychotic, vicious creature that should under any normal circumstances be cuddled comfortably in a plaid, flannel dog bed surrounded by adoring family with ruddy-faced children before a blazing fire. It seems they can't even buy any toys for Cujo, because he simply eats them, I mean completely! They have never found Warren's bowling ball, which disappeared last year and sends my imagination reeling.

Everyone else in the building is aware of Cujo and his violent nature. Window blinds can often be seen cracking open before residents venture outside, as though they need to make sure Cujo is nowhere in sight first. At times it appears that this fifteen-pound dog is holding our building hostage and that the world's fear of Pit Bulls is entirely misplaced, when indeed, all the Pit Bulls I've met have been sweet-natured, playful dogs, totally unlike the unfair and inaccurate stereotype created because a few morons have bred them for fighting. As a dog lover, I feel awful that in rare cases like that of Cujo the Boston Terrorist, the dog cannot be peacefully and lovingly approached. Cujo has made me perhaps unnecessarily wary around new dogs, for the first time in my life. In any case, maybe I can blame his unsociable behavior on a Napoleon Complex. I mean, have you ever met a mean St. Bernard or Great Dane?

Chapter 37: Friendships

The value of true friendships is probably inestimable. Lasting friendships anchor us in a world that is changing ever faster each year. Those friendships give us a shared history of experiences from good and bad times, because friends have seen each other at their best and at their worst. They know each other's strengths and weaknesses but are able to extol those strengths over the weaknesses, so that forgiveness always triumphs over any possible grudges. As we continue to age, sometimes our children and our friends move away (or we do), but the old bonds remain in place as bulwarks of our relationships with our shared pasts. Friendships never stop being vital parts of life.

Our hair may whiten with the years, as

Microsoft programs come and go, and gas prices continue to rise higher than those we used to pay for fine jewelry, but our good friends are able to keep a sense of continuity and meaning in our lives. Whenever we ask, "Do you remember?" about something or someone from forty or fifty years before, the smile of recollection on the friend's face as he answers, "Yes, I remember" means we are not alone. We have something together that no amount of money can buy, because we are connected by reminiscences, even when they become the only ones left to stave off the slow approach of dementia or the oblivion of Alzheimer's.

As the years roll by, the number of friends with whom we share remembrances shrinks, like the old clothes from college that no longer fit us and have been tossed into the attic. Our perspectives shrink too, until there is no one remaining, who remembers what we remember. The old friend with whom I took the wrong train and ended up in Cleveland when we were in high school together may be the last to laugh at that private recollection.

As someone who has moved across the country twice during the past six years, I know the enormous significance of dear friends I have left behind, even though we are still in regular contact by phone, computer, and occasional visits. Our dearest friends cannot be replaced by better climate, a lovelier home, or increased financial opportunities. Friends are the "family" we choose. They are our mainstay, our stability, our safeguard in a world that is spinning faster year by year toward ever more impersonal, electronic communication, and mere "virtual" relationships as disposable as plastic water bottles. If we do nothing else of importance during our golden years, it should be to value and nurture those friendships that are the best ones, often the oldest (while continuing to make new ones), along with all the shared laughter and tears that they provide.

Chapter 38: Tribute to My Sister, Connie Lynn Bolinger

My sister Connie lived in a very private world, usually keeping people, even those closest to her, at a respectful distance, not because she didn't love them, but rather because she felt that any problems she might be carrying should never weigh down those around her, and opening those locked doors meant releasing pain she did not want to share with others even if it signified receiving the regard and healing that those around her often wanted so much to give her. Part of this, of course, was based upon Connie's fierce pride in her own independence, but part came also from her staunch personal resolution never to wound anyone with her own burdens.

The place where my sister found peace, beauty, and healing was in music. That is where the material world dissolved for her through seeing new harmonies and breathtaking melodies. Anyone who ever found the real Connie discovered her there, where musical invention came from her speaking to God and from God's responses through Connie's heart and down through her fingers at the keyboard.

My sister had a short temper and could, with little provocation, verbally julienne someone like a cat shredding window drapes. But, she also had a wonderful sense of humor, a generous heart, and a faith in God not often shaken, even by the enormous trials she faced.

I remember holding my sister in the little pink

blanket used to bring her home from the hospital after her birth. I was seven years old. We became over time each other's chief promoter and protector, and now that I will miss her, I am thankful for the fifty-eight years of memories we shared together. Thank God for Connie.

Recently Connie gave me a copy of the poem "On Playing Church Piano," which she said expressed perfectly what she felt each time she sat at the keyboard in this place.

On Playing a Church Piano

It's something about the darkness of the place,
when I relax a moment to decide what makes
this work so pleasing; is it the thrill of lights
fixed on the tall bronze cross, or perhaps the

colored figures in the glass? But then the stack of staves upon the stand cries out for study, and my fingers arch again and dance, though not gracefully at first -- more like cautious children avoiding creaky boards. Yet hidden strings in the wood awake and sing -- and the dark, cool room seems full. And then I realize: It is.

Chapter 39: Words from the Old to the Young

I would like to provide as a conclusion to this book a brief commentary by John Tapene, president of Northland College, who in an address to the student body quoted the words of a judge who regularly dealt with teenagers, who in their perpetual boredom asked "What can we do and where can we go?" We've all encountered that attitude among young people, who expect us to show them the way by building the road for them, complete with signposts and entertainment along the way. The judge's response was:

"My answer is this: Go home, mow the lawn, wash the windows, learn to cook, build a raft, get a job, visit the sick, study your lessons, and after you've finished, read a book. Your town does not owe you recreational facilities, and your parents do not owe you fun.

The world does not owe you a living. You owe the world something. You owe it your time, energy and talent so that no one will be at war, in sickness and lonely again. In other words grow up, stop being a cry baby, get out of your dream world and develop a backbone not a wishbone. Start behaving like a responsible person. You are important and you are needed. It's too late to sit around and wait for somebody to do something someday. Someday is now, and that somebody is you!"

It seems appropriate for us who are in our golden years to pass the torch to younger generations. Aging doesn't have to be the nightmare it is often portrayed to be in the media. Growing old is natural and can be done with grace and aplomb, and what makes it seem less painful is that so many of us can grow old together in mutual support of whatever problems we may have to face along the way. My favorite comedian was always Jack Benny. When he turned 39 years old, he never aged again, always celebrating his 39th birthday for the rest of his life. Maybe age is how we feel, not just a number. My book has thirty-nine chapters. Here's to you, Jack!

John Bolinger

June 10, 2014

65423026R00139

Made in the USA
Charleston, SC
26 December 2016